A SUPPLEMENTAL ISSUE TO

RON THE WRITER:
THE SHAPING OF POPULAR FICTION

A SUPPLEMENTAL ISSUE TO

RON THE WRITER:
THE SHAPING OF POPULAR FICTION

L. RON HUBBARD

LETTERS AND JOURNALS

LITERARY
CORRESPONDENCE

...to write, writ[e]
then write some m[ore]
And never to all[ow]
weariness, lack
time, noise, or
other thing to t[urn]
me off my course[.]

CONTENTS

ISBN 1-57318-130-7

© 1997 L. Ron Hubbard Library. All Rights Reserved.

Dianetics, Scientology, LRH, the Ron Signature and the LRH Signet are trademarks and service marks owned by Religious Technology Center and are used with its permission.

Background photographs appearing on pages 4–5, 8–9, 10, 14–15, 16–17, 22–23, 36, 37, 40–41, 42–43, 44–45, 46–47, 54–55, 56–57, 58–59, 60–61, 62–63, 64–65, 66–67, 68–69, 70–71, 72–73, 74–75, courtesy American Stock Photography. Background photographs appearing on pages 18–19, 20–21, courtesy National Geographic Society. Photograph of Robert Heinlein appearing on page 84, courtesy J. K. Klien.

John W. Campbell, Jr. letters of January 23, 1939; March 21, 1939; and April 19, 1939 appearing on pages 25–27 reproduced by permission of AC Projects, Inc., Franklin, TN 37064.

An Introductory Note

From the greater body of materials assembled for the eventual L. Ron Hubbard biography and that augmentative biographical project, the Ron Series, comes an extensive collection of LRH correspondence and journals. All told, this collection constitutes a remarkable find, providing much detail and color to a most remarkable life. Given these papers span the whole of that life—from the earliest steps of Ron's journey to his ultimate triumph—this issue marks yet another in a new series of supplemental Ron publications, *Ron: Letters and Journals*. As the term "supplemental" implies, Letters and Journals are intended to be read in conjunction with the Ron Series. For in providing extracts of materials from which the Ron Series is derived, readers receive both a feel of the time and a sense of Ron's voice through the various phases of his life discussed in that series.

True, what is presented here represents but a fraction of the material from which the Ron Series is distilled. Indeed, beneath the Ron Series proper and the LRH biography stand more than a hundred-thousand pages of LRH letters, journals and diaries. Yet given the insight even a small selection of these materials offer, Letters and Journals become invaluable. For example, much has been previously said regarding Ron's role in the shaping of popular American literature through the 1930s, with such immediately memorable tales as *Buckskin Brigades*, *Death's Deputy* and *Final Blackout*—well, here is the to-and-from with editors of those tales and correspondence with colleagues while pondering plots and characterization.

With an eye to providing that same sense of the moment, Letters and Journals have presented correspondence from Ron's early years of adventure, the founding of Dianetics and critical notes from his road to research.

THE LITERARY CORRESPONDENCE OF L. RON HUBBARD

Presented in this publication is a significant selection of correspondence from the literary life of L. Ron Hubbard. Although a full appreciation of that life is only possible from a reading of the companion to this publication, *Ron the Writer: The Shaping of Popular Fiction*, let us at least consider the broader strokes.

Long synonymous with high adventure and far-flung exploration, the name L. Ron Hubbard originally graced the pages of some two hundred rough-stock periodicals, otherwise known as the pulps and likewise synonymous with raw adventure in exotic locales. Included among his more than fifteen million words of pre-1950 fiction were tales spanning all primary genres: action, intrigue, mysteries, westerns, even the occasional romance. Enlisted to "humanize" a machine-dominated science fiction, the name L. Ron Hubbard next became synonymous with such utterly classic titles as *Final Blackout* and *To The Stars*—rightfully described as among the most defining works in the whole of the genre. No less memorable were his fantasies of the era, including the perennially applauded *Fear*, described as a pillar of all modern horror. Indeed, as the critics tell us, there is finally no speculative writer of note—from Ray Bradbury to Stephen King—who does not owe a literary debt to the early tales of L. Ron Hubbard.

With the founding of Dianetics and Scientology (the fruition of research actually financed through those fifteen million words of fiction), Ron withdrew from the literary arena for some thirty years . . . Whereupon he returned to the field in the early 1980s with two monumental blockbusters: the internationally best-selling *Battlefield Earth,* and the ten-volume *Mission Earth* (each volume likewise topping international bestseller lists in what amounted to an unprecedented publishing event). Thereafter, and with worldwide sales of LRH novels approaching forty million, we come to the real appeal of this publication: the letters of an author who now stands among the most influential, enduring and widely read authors of the twentieth century.

In one way or another, the letters here illuminate all we have so briefly sketched. From a hopeful winter of 1934, comes a precious hundred dollars courtesy of an Ed Bodin literary agent to a host of desperate authors fighting for a place in that keenly competitive pulp-fiction market. From a somewhat healthier summer of 1935, comes Ron's formal greeting to readers of *Adventure* as "a tall red-haired chap with a service background." From an altogether prosperous 1936, comes the editorial back-and-forth for a first full-length novel, while Florence McChesney of *Five Novels Monthly* wonders "if you're doing a flying story for me next." Then follows a contemplative exchange of notes on characterization, an equally contemplative sequence from a thoughtful season in Manhattan and several wry words on fencing with irascible editors. While very much to the point of the troublesome editor, comes a choice selection of letters to-and-from John W. Campbell, Jr. on the reshaping of speculative fiction despite John W. Campbell.

The greater point: For all we have seen in explanation of L. Ron Hubbard's literary triumph, here is the deepest view yet. Here is the huddling with editors to firmly lay down story lines, then the "wondering what the hell they'll find wrong this time, certain that it will be different than the last." Here is that "jittery frame of mind" at the first blank page, and "all the fun I want in twisting plots and trying out stunts of technique." Here is the crafting of tales to satisfy the banker, plumber, bellhop and grocer—all while striving for perfection, "because if we achieve perfection then we have come as close to the activity of the self as a mortal can get." In short, here is the literary life of an author as only an author can express it, and then only to another who lives it.

In addition to personal correspondence as such, we include Ron's 1936 open letter to New York columnist O. O. McIntyre in defense of the pulps, his equally open advice to "word weary" fledglings and the transcription of his radio discussion with Ed Bodin and Arthur J. Burks, a.k.a. "Mr. Pulps" himself. We further include his letters in farewell to the pulps from 1949, his notes to Robert Heinlein upon returning to a literary life in the 1980s, and much else relating to what followed from the very crucial, ". . . and then, by god, I'll write."

Editors, Manuscripts and the Business of Writing

"I was born in Nebraska and three weeks later went to Oklahoma," or so L. Ron Hubbard introduced himself to the no-nonsense readers of *Adventure*. To what he supplies in the way of his thumbnail sketch, let us add the following: His initial submissions had been furiously pounded out through a six-week stint following his return from a Puerto Rican mining expedition. He wrote blind—which is to say, without benefit of editorial direction—and submitted to the slush pile—which is to say, without benefit of known representation. Nevertheless, he managed to net himself half-a-dozen crucial sales by the end of 1933, whereupon he joined the stable of agent Ed Bodin and the "regular contributor" lists of such top-line publications as *Five Novels Monthly* and *Argosy*. Then, too, and given no issue would carry more than a single story from any one author, he had further launched the careers of Ken Martin and Lt. Jonathan Daly, i.e., the first of several LRH pen names and thus the point of Bodin's letter of late 1934. That is, Leo Margulies of Standard Magazines had apparently purchased an anonymous story so plainly smacking of L. Ron Hubbard he immediately suspected a plagiarizing hand. In fact, L. Ron Hubbard had penned that story, but Bodin had removed the byline, (presumably to place the tale in an issue already featuring LRH). In either case, here is the Bodin suggestion of a "Legionnaire Longworth," which, in turn, became "Legionnaire 148," and thus the later pen name of several LRH adventures with French colonial settings.

Also pursuant to this business of writing comes the classic back-and-forth on plots and money with the likes of Florence McChesney of *Five Novels Monthly* and a William Kostka of *Detective Fiction Weekly*. Then again, we come to the equally classic LRH-Jack Byrne exchange on *Buckskin Brigades* and the same again with *Unknown* and *Astounding Science Fiction* editor John W. Campbell, Jr.

The point being: although popularly described as an aristocrat of high adventure or a leading light of science fiction, L. Ron Hubbard actually wrote them all: two-fisted westerns, white-knuckled thrillers, brooding mysteries and even the occasional heart-throbber for Miss Fanny Ellsworth's *Ranch Romances*.

ASSOCIATE EDITOR
THE WRITER'S REVIEW
CINCINNATI, OHIO

NATIONAL SECRETARY 1934
AMERICAN FICTION GUILD

EDITOR "THE MANUSCRIPT MAN" COLUMN
BIRMINGHAM NEWS-AGE-HERALD
BIRMINGHAM, ALA.

MARKET-TIP COLUMNIST
CALIFORNIA ART NEWS

FORMER NEWSPAPER COLUMNS:
LETTERS TO LUCIFER
WEEKLY NUMBERSCOPE
ED BODIN'S EDITORIAL

ED BODIN
AUTHOR'S EXECUTIVE
151 FIFTH AVENUE
NEW YORK CITY

11 YEARS WITH PUBLISHERS OF
COLLIER'S
AMERICAN MAGAZINE
WOMEN'S HOME COMPANION
COUNTRY HOME

TELEPHONES:
ALGONQUIN 4-3310
ALGONQUIN 4-6171

December 26, 1934

Dear Hubbard:

Here's the deep dark secret which you will have to keep mum on your life. In other words, don't dare tell Leo or anyone that you are the author of that story you sent me.

I took it up to Leo and told him here was a writer who had to keep his name secret for alimony reasons and that I could deliver him more material from the same pen.

This morning he called me up and wanted to know if it was a plagiarism for it was a damn good yarn, but the best he could offer was $100. I told him to send the check. Then he wanted to know who the author was and if he had ever heard of him. All I said, I would guarantee on my own rep that it wasn't a plagiarism and that I was pledged to secrecy on the name and couldn't tell my own mother.

Suppose you give me some pen name to keep in my files as I don't want to keep the docket on you in your own name in case one of my assistants should spill the beans, someday accidently. This would sour Leo toward me too.

Frankly, I'd like to get you into LIBERTY on some adventure stuff. I've sold LIBERTY over 50,000 words of adventure within the last few weeks. How about a name like Legionnaire Longworth, or some name we could build.

But of course, that's up to you. Just keep it mum that I have any of your stuff and someday the story of your secret trail will make good reading.

Respectfully,

Ed Bodin

Ed Bodin, Ron's literary agent through much of the 1930s.

Adventure

POPULAR PUBLICATIONS, Inc.
205 East 42nd Street, New York, N. Y.

July 24, 1935
L. Ron Hubbard, Esq.
Cannondale, Conn.

Dear Hubbard:

In looking over your autobiographical notes, I
wish you had been more explicit about the Marine
experience and other experiences.

All you fellows get a little self-conscious when
you write about yourselves, and I wish you would do
this over in a more definite and serious vein and
mail it tomorrow, so that I will have it Friday to
send to the printers.

Much obliged—and good luck.

Sincerely,

Howard Bloomfield
Editor

Vol. 93. No. 5   October 1, 1935   Twice A Month

THE CAMP-FIRE

*where readers, writers
and adventurers
meet*

L Ron Hubbard joins our Writers'
Brigade with his leatherneck yarn,
"He Walked to War." Hubbard is a tall
red-haired chap with a service background, his father being an officer. He
introduces himself at the Camp-Fire. —
Howard V. L. Bloomfield, Editor.

I was born in Nebraska and three weeks
later went to Oklahoma. From there to
Missouri, then to Montana. When I was a
year old, they say I showed some signs of
settling down, but I think this is merely
rumor. Changing locales from the Pacific
Coast to the Atlantic Coast every few
months, it was not until I was almost
twelve that I first left the United States.
And it was not until I was sixteen that I
headed for the China Coast.

In spite of changing schools, I received
an education. I have some very poor
grade sheets which show that I studied to
be a civil engineer in college.

Civil engineering seemed very handsome
at the time. I met the lads in their Stetsons
from Crabtown to Timbuktu and they
seemed to lead a very colorful existence
squinting into their transits. However, too
late, I was sent up to Maine by the
Geological Survey to find the lost Canadian
Border. Much bitten by seven kinds of
insects, gummed by the muck of swamps,
fed on johnny cake[1] and tarheel,[2] I saw
instantly that a civil engineer had to stay
far too long in far too few places and so I
rapidly forgot my calculus and slip stick
and began to plot ways and means to avoid
the continuance of my education. I decided
on an expedition into the Caribbean.

It was a crazy idea at best and I knew it,
but I went ahead anyway, chartered a
four-masted schooner and embarked with
some fifty luckless souls who haven't
ceased their cursings yet. Our present
generation just doesn't take to salt horse,

1. johnny cake: corn bread baked on a griddle.
2. tarheel: thick syrup made of molasses and maple syrup.

dried peas, and a couple quarts of water a day.

But the expedition did the trick. I did not have to return to college. Instead I returned to the West Indies.

I might remark upon a coincidence which has always amazed me. While in the West Indies I discovered signs of gold on an island and, harboring the thought that the conquistadores might have left some gold behind, I determined to find it.

. . . After half a year or more of intensive search, after wearing my palms thin wielding a sample pick, after assaying a few hundred sacks of ore, I came back, a failure.

But a month after my return to Maryland, I discovered a vein of honey-comb quartz in the back pasture. The body of ore was tremendous, the visible vein several yards wide at the narrowest. Under the $20.67[3] an ounce, it assayed $82.34 a ton, and it is now worth about $145 a ton. However, to mine it takes money and I would have to stay close to Maryland. It's still there.

Chronological narration, in this short sketch, is impossible. Therefore, permit me to jump about a bit.

I was once convinced that the future of aviation lies in motorless flight. Accordingly I started gliding and soaring with the rest of the buzzards, and finally succeeded in establishing a record which has no official existence whatever and no reason, indeed, for existing. I traveled better than eighty miles an hour for twelve minutes in a soaring plane, maintaining the same altitude about an airport which is set on a flat plain. Answer: Heat lift from the circling concrete road.

From there I went into power flight, the high spot of which came on a barnstorming trip through the Midwest in a five-lunged[4] crate which staggered rather than flew. All one summer, I tried very hard to meet St. Pete, but evidently that gentleman either lost my name from the roll or my luck is far better than I think it is.

Unfortunately, in my Asiatic wanderings, no one, not even Hindu fortunetellers, thought to inform me that I would someday make my living with a typewriter and so I completely forgot to conduct myself informatively and devoted my time to enjoying life.

In Peiping, for instance, I did not avail myself of photographic impressions I might well have gained. I completely missed the atmosphere of the city, devoting most of my time to a British major who happened to be head of the Intelligence out there.

3. The price of an ounce of gold circa 1935.

4. five-lunged: five-cylindered.

In Shanghai, I am ashamed to admit that I did not tour the city or surrounding country as I should have. I know more about 181 Bubbling Wells Road and its wheels[5] than I do about the history of the town.

In Hong Kong... well, why take up space?

Time after time, people accuse me of having been in the Marines. Pushed right up against the wall, I am forced to admit a connection with that very cosmopolitan outfit, however short lived and vague. I was once a top-kicker[6] in the 20th because, as they sing in Shin-ho,

I walked down the street
Without a cent in my jeans,
And that is the reason
I joined the Marines.

I am not sure that calling squads east and west fits a man for writing, but it does give him a vocabulary.

One thing I might mention in connection with the leathernecks, most of the fiction written about them is of an intensely dramatic type, all do and die and *semper fidelis* and the dear old flag.

To me the Marine Corps is a more go-to-hell outfit than the much-lauded French Foreign Legion ever could be. The two are comparable in many ways. God knows what you'll find in either, from college professors to bellhops. Just why the disappointed lover has to sneak off for North Africa all the time is a riddle. More men have taken refuge in the Corps than in the Legion and, judging from association, leathernecks certainly lead a sufficiently exciting existence.

I've known the Corps from Quantico to Peiping, from the South Pacific to the West Indies, and I've never seen any flag-waving. The most refreshing part of the USMC is that they get their orders and start out and do the job and that's that. Whether that job was to storm the heights of Chapultepec so that the United States Army could proceed, or to dislodge a crazy gentleman named John Brown from an arsenal at Harpers Ferry, or to knock off a few Boxers for the glory of England, your Marine went and did the job and then retired to bind up his wounds while everyone else went on parade.

Let it suffice. This is more than a thumbnail sketch, but I hope it's a passport to your interest. I know a lot of you out there, and I haven't heard from you in years. I know I haven't had any address, but I'm certain the editor will forward my mail.

When I get back from Central America, where I'm going soon, I'll have another yarn to tell.

L. Ron Hubbard

---

5. wheels: reference to wheels of gambling machines, i.e., the roulette wheel.
6. top-kicker: first sergeant; drill sergeant.

DELL PUBLISHING COMPANY, INC.
149 MADISON AVENUE
NEW YORK

GEORGE T. DELACORTE, JR.
PRESIDENT

CABLE ADDRESS "DELLPUB"

360 N. MICHIGAN AVE.
CHICAGO, ILL.

October 16, 1936

Dear Ron:

Okay for "The Renegades." It's wild, but not too wild. The main thing is that the story has "it"—appeal to readers, without insulting their intelligence. Next on the book is the popular yarn of the air. I haven't had any readers' comment on "Sky Birds Dare!" but if the readers don't like that, I disown them . . . it was a darn good story.

I see that a British publisher is anxious to back a flight rivaling the American publishers' Around-the-World affair, which has been getting large publicity. And I wonder if you couldn't write a whale of a good air yarn about international rivals on a flight like that. Keep the American-British or whatever angle clean straight sportsmanship, so far as the backers are concerned, but drag in a lot of dirty work by unscrupulous guys on one side or the other—preferably both. However, don't let the suggestion cramp your style. Write what you please. Air is the idea . . . and you do it darn well. Whatever you do, keep the next story in mind—the Alaskan yarn, which I'm counting on. I rather thought you could use flying in it, but if you're doing a flying story for me next, maybe the flying in the Alaskan yarn had better be incidental. And so—anyway, let me know what you propose to do. . . .

By the way, both Reynolds and Scruggs are entering the Little-Brown novelette contest, not with too optimistic an eye on the prizes, but with hopes of being bought for publication anyway. Are you competing? I think the length runs between about 15,000 and 35,000—short novel length.

Adios for now.

With all good wishes,

Florence

Mr. L. Ron Hubbard
44th Street Hotel
New York City

February 1, 1937
1212 Gregory Way
Bremerton, Wash.

Florence McChesney
Editor, FIVE NOVELS
149 Madison Ave.
New York City

Dear Florence;

Herewith enclosed is VANGUARD TO STEEL. As you are the prize titleer, I have let the working title stick.

Ahead of me I have a long line of syllables but now that I've turned this one out for you I can attack them in a little better frame of mind. For two reasons: I didn't wholly let you down and there's always the chance of a check for it. These reasons are both very powerful.

Writing long stuff is all right, especially when you have received an advance. But when there is a tie-up on a novel, the poor writer, who has done nothing but work on it suddenly discovers that he has neglected his regular markets and is momentarily in a financial slump. This seems to be the danger of novels. No wonder the boys treat them with fear and trembling and also with curled lips. Leave it to the Hollywood lawyers to put a red flag in front of the check line by way of contract clauses.

I hear tell you're having a most warm winter. Out here, of all things, it has snowed steadily for weeks—unheard of in this country. I wonder if Roosevelt didn't shift the climate around too.

I thought I was coming to New York and then I thought I was coming and now I don't know what to think. So I don't think any more than I have to. I work and hope for the best.

This only seems to prove that no matter how far afield I may stray, I'll probably always be going around muttering to myself, "Gee, I think it's about time I did one for Florence." You don't know how comfortable it is to look back at the record book and know that the backbone of my career is FIVE NOVELS. Through long experience I can usually read the manuscript, think it over and then predict success or failure. Such steadiness of decision and such even choice is a feather in your cap. For most editors I write in a very jittery frame of mind, wondering what the hell they'll find wrong this time, certain that it will be different than the last. Which is probably the reason your lads work so faithfully and steadily for you.

Although rates do make a difference, most of your writers will keep on with the editor who is the most consistent in reports because that way lies a comfortable peace of mind.

For instance your one remark has been, on actual style, that sometimes I would get confused in who was doing what. I pay particular attention to that now. Your comment on plot was that my yarns are sometimes wild. I have been slowly cutting down the improbability and I want to know when I reach a normal level. Outside of this, there isn't anything to keep me up in the air about what to do next.

I do not mean to intimate that I am smugly satisfied as to an assured acceptance. Far from that. But I know you won't throw one back at me unless you have very definite reasons—the fact which marks the good editor. No flattery that, because it is backed by the way Bruner and Scruggs and Holmes and Reynolds and I stick to our twenty-thousand worders for FIVE NOVELS. I know of no other magazine which is able to keep a consistent array of material.

If you want to know how you have improved my style and smoothed my work, compare, for instance, THE BRAVE DARE ALL and SEA FANGS. And there's plenty of room between the former and some future story.

Ah, well, wish I could drop in and cuss and discuss things with you.

Best regards,

Ron

Ron

Thrilling Adventures
Thrilling Detective
Thrilling Love
Thrilling Ranch Stories
Thrilling Western
Sky Fighters
The Lone Eagle
The Phantom Detective
Popular Western
Popular Detective

STANDARD MAGAZINES, Inc.
22 WEST 48th STREET
NEW YORK

Cable Address
"MAGSTAND"

Leo Margulies, editor at Standard Magazines.

February 26, 1935

Mr. L. Ron Hubbard
222 Riverside Drive
New York City

Dear Ron:

There's a gaping hole in the inventory of THRILLING ADVENTURES that just must be filled.

The requirements are simple—a fast moving action story, locale, any spot on earth. Nothing barred—from westerns, pseudo-scientific, detective, costume to the good old-fashioned he-man American soldier-of-fortune running amuck around the world.

And all lengths—from two thousand word short-shorts to twenty thousand word novelettes. And we have no taboos because of an odd length.

We'll pay one cent a word—with a quick decision and prompt payment on acceptance.

Have you anything on hand to shoot along?

Sincerely yours,
LEO MARGULIES
Editorial Director

LRH

December 7, 1937
Route One, Box 452
Port Orchard, Wash.

Miss Fanny Ellsworth
Editor, RANCH ROMANCES
515 Madison Ave.
New York City

Dear Miss Ellsworth;

I send you ROBIN HOOD OF THE RANGE.[1] I would like very much to have your reaction to this story so that I can angle others more closely.

In the past, Ed Bodin sent a few strays your way but I have no way of knowing your comment on them and Bodin is no longer handling my stories.[2]

Best regards,

L. Ron Hubbard

1. Eventually retitled "When Gilhooly Was in Flower," and appearing in the August 1938 issue of _Romantic Range_.
2. In the autumn of 1937, under wholly amicable circumstances, LRH left the Bodin stable to represent himself. Although he would never advertise the reasons for his departure, we know the agent had long lacked the wherewithal to routinely market subsidiary rights in Hollywood and abroad.

Route 1, Box 452
Port Orchard, Wash.
April 22, 1937

Mr. William Kostka
Editor, DETECTIVE FICTION WEEKLY
280 Broadway
New York City

Dear Mr. Kostka;

Enclosed, find FANGS OF THE TIGER,[1] 10,500 word novelette which I tailored for DFW on the pattern of the stories I used to write for your excellent book.

Due to the press of other affairs, I have not submitted a story to DFW for over six months, but as I expect to have a clear slate ahead, even while south this spring, this lack of good sense on my part will be compensated to the best of my ability.

Unfortunately I have been stuck on this coast for eight months, doing long stuff, and I have gotten entirely out of contact with my markets except through the able hands of Mr. Ed Bodin, my agent, who should receive the report on this story. If there is any particular type of story you wish and if there is anything in my repertoire you would like, I would be very flattered to hear from you.

So abysmal has my ignorance been that I had to phone Frank Pierce this morning to confirm the welcome news that you were the editor, and that I overlooked such a pleasant fact is demonstrative of the depth of my hermit's retreat. I mention this only in order that I may extend my belated best wishes and to apologize for not sending them sooner.

Hoping that you will find this latest effort of mine worthy of both your interest and your book and hoping also that it is at least good enough to invite further contacts on stories, I am

Sincerely,

L. Ron Hubbard

1. Owing to William Kostka's foreshortened stay at Detective Fiction Weekly (actually under four weeks), he was not to publish "Fangs of the Tiger." The hard-boiled pages of Detective Yarns, however, was soon to see a similarly intriguing LRH mystery, "Killer Ape."

On "Buckskin Brigades"

Inspired by Ron's youthful encounters with the Blackfeet of Montana, *Buckskin Brigades* would finally prove the most celebrated of all L. Ron Hubbard westerns. Described as a "vigorously authentic" tale "told through the mind and body of the American Indian," the story ultimately chronicles the tragic encounter between a then mighty Blackfoot nation and an avaricious Hudson Bay Company. Eventually published as a full-length novel from The Macaulay Company, *Buckskin Brigades* would enjoy an extraordinarily long shelf life with extended critical acclaim for more than fifty years. While the work still lay in progress, however, Ron had toyed with the possibilities of serialization in Jack Byrne's *Argosy*. That Byrne eventually declined is, of course, incidental to Ron's thoughts on the matter and Byrne's oh-so-typical editorial input.

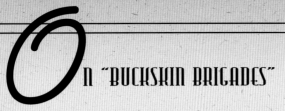

THE FRANK A. MUNSEY COMPANY
280 BROADWAY
NEW YORK
Members
ALL FICTION FIELD

Argosy
Detective Fiction

All-Story
Railroad Stories

November 27, 1936

Mr. L. Ron Hubbard
1212 Gregory Way
Bremerton, Washington

My dear Hubbard:

I'm glad to hear that you are interested in the serial because I have a hunch that you are going to do us a good yarn on this one. "Buckskin Brigades" is a very good title, I think.

I agree with you about the regular western fiction which fills so many of our magazines. These yarns as a whole are pretty dull stuff, it seems to me. I like to think of our ARGOSY Westerns now as historical yarns. I believe too that the majority of adult readers in the field are also chiefly interested in historical aspects. Wherefore we can kill two birds by giving them the real thing as far as background goes and still develop the colorful fiction story in the bargain.

Let me know how your work progresses when you get a chance. Our ARGOSY sales have been showing a little pickup as you know, but we fell into a slump during the election period after seeming to be on our way in September. I think we are building solidly though and that we will keep on showing progress as we go along.

Best of luck,

Jack Byrne
Editor
ARGOSY

1212 Gregory Way
Bremerton, Wash.
December 8, 1936

Mr. Jack Byrne
Editor
ARGOSY
280 Broadway
New York City

Dear Mr. Byrne;

Enclosed is the synopsis of BUCKSKIN BRIGADES.

Except for a few minor plot changes which are always bound to
creep into the actual writing as you well know, this is the way
she goes.

It is carefully planned for effect more than anything else,
and I think it will make a racy yarn. As a glance will tell you,
it is based upon characters, not plot alone.

I have pooled the most exciting events of the fur trade and
these, in their turn, have of course influenced the time
spacing.

Apparently the beginning is a little slow, but for the sake of
brevity I have omitted the form and have simply stated the
facts. Cutbacks and inter-plot will speed it up.

As you wished, this will probably run between sixty and
seventy thousand words as there will be no lack of suspense and
interest and the subject, in all fairness to it, demands much
more. . . .

Probably you will wonder a little at the ending I have jotted
here. Without this ending the whole structure will lean in the
trite direction taken by so many costume novels.[1] It is impossible
to see that in this short summary which follows and in spite of
what most writers seem to think, clairvoyance isn't a part of an
editorial job. And so, as it will come out in its proper length,
my idea, condensed, is this: The Indian in his backwoods was much
better off without any contact on the turbulent white frontier,
beset as it was with the turbulence of the fur brigades.

I am not yet satisfied with my research as several inquiries I
have made to well-known ethnologists and friends up on Indian lore
have not yet been returned to me. However, this is all pertinent to
weapons, costume, hunting methods and woodcraft—small points, but
very vital to the life thread of such a work.

I am also enclosing an airmail envelope for the return as I
hope to start on this not later than the coming Sunday at which
time I will have assembled everything, rolled up my sleeves,
bought a new ribbon, emitted a war-whoop preparatory to getting
into the spirit of the thing. . . .

Best regards,

L. Ron Hubbard

---

1. costume novel: a historical novel with authentic characters, scenes and descriptions.

THE FRANK A. MUNSEY COMPANY

280 BROADWAY

NEW YORK

Members
ALL FICTION FIELD

Argosy
Detective Fiction

All-Story
Railroad Stories

December 11, 1936

Mr. L. Ron Hubbard
1212 Gregory Way
Bremerton, Wash.

Dear Hubbard:

I see a great deal of promise in the material you have outlined for
"Buckskin Brigades." As you can understand, I am not particularly concerned
right now with the plot motion of the story or the incidents thereof: I know
that you can handle these and weld them together into a harmonious whole. I
do, however, like your people and the general situation. My chief injunction
now is this: remember that you are selling a fiction story against a historical
background; don't let things that have actually happened obstruct the free
use of your imagination and the dramatization of what might have been.

A secondary point to watch is to see that we get the individual emotional
reaction of the other characters as well as that of the hero to a certain
extent. For instance, White Fox should not trail Yellow Hair with unalloyed
beneficence, it seems to me. He should dislike certain tendencies the
youngster shows, be deeply resentful of the fact that Michael is so aroused
by the white girl when Little Star is waiting for him. I think too that
Little Star should be quite a character--a warrior woman rather than a girl
who waits complacently to be taken when our hero returns from the wars.

I also sense (I may be wrong on this) that there is need for additional
personal problems as far as Michael is concerned. This is merely offhand
suggestion, but it occurred to me that in one of his early contacts with the
whites, the leader of the whites would sense the potential value of this
young fellow to his faction. He would get Michael drunk and have him take
part in the attack against another faction in which various whites would be
killed. Thus Michael wakes up in the morning with scalps at his belt and
with his new found friends telling him of the terrific battle he has put up.
He has no memory of it and must perforce accept their story as the truth.
This, of course, will mean that if Michael is captured by the rivals he will
immediately be drawn and quartered; and that his reputation as a tough son-
of-a-gun goes throughout the country. This would be a factor against him in
the eyes of Evelyn Lee. It would also give him an additional problem to
solve, etc.

I note too a sort of tendency to have him rescued from various jams and
captures by talking his way out or through the intercedence of a third
party. Why not let him instead make spectacular daring escapes that would be
in keeping with his character as the fastest running, the swiftest and
truest arrow, the lightest man among the Blackfeet? When Take-Gun-Twice
captures him, for example, why can he not outdo the great Iroquois in
various Indian tests of strength and skill so that Take-Gun-Twice would
first have to kill Michael before he can again claim to be the strongest
and bravest among all the red men as was his boast.

I am just shooting these arrows into the air as offhand suggestions.
The purpose of them being merely to stimulate your thinking along the
lines they indicate. Otherwise, I think everything shapes up excellently
and I'll be very interested to see how the story works out.

Why not let me look at the first installment or the first two
installments, say, when you have finished it. I might have some ideas
that I could send along to you at that time which would be of assistance.

Sincerely,

Jack Byrne
Editor
ARGOSY

Old Tom, Blackfoot
medicine man who
honored a young
L. Ron Hubbard with
that very rare status
of blood brother.

1212 Gregory Way
Bremerton, Wash.
January 18, 1937

Dear Mr. Byrne;

...It was fine of you to speed up your reading on BUCKSKIN BRIGADES in view of the stacks of manuscripts through which you daily have to swim and burn up a weekend as well.

Stage fright is a recognized mental state, but syllable-scare ought to have its place in psychiatry. I guess I could have turned out that story hand over fist for any cheap market in the field, but when it came to placing it before you and ARGOSY I can tell you I didn't get much sleep while I was writing it. It was only after I really dug into the story for the story itself that I managed to partially shake off my jitters. In trying to make the grade I gave it a theme and an entirely different pattern and was altogether too intent upon pioneering a new type of frontier story to remember that, after all, it had to be read as well as written. And when I added palsy ...

Oh well, you haven't got time for excuses. All you want is results.

I have a story here now, ready to start, which will run sixty thousand and should take six weeks in the writing. Africa. Plenty of excitement in it and a couple unusual characters. . . .

And please don't be too tough on me for BUCKSKIN BRIGADES because you know yourself that a writer is slam-bang up against his story and even though he is living it, thrilling to it, slaving on it, he very often fails to know whether the story is good or bad after he has finished it. I guess that was the case this time. When I was very young at this business I accepted my own reaction. But I've had too many I thought were bad accepted as good and too many good accepted as bad until I finally began to realize that, regardless of my capabilities, my knowledge of worth was too small for a second consideration. And now I carefully reserve my own judgment on anything and everything in spite of the effort put forth until someone who really knows about these things hands out sentence. An unhappy state of mind, I know, and one which, at first glance, might be considered servile. It is not.

And so, I don't think you'll find me guilty of any bitterness on any decision and as I am more interested in the truth than my feelings in the matter. After all, I only know my technique and have only had to develop craftsmanship. You were made responsible for the destiny of Munsey because you have proved over a long period that you are a past master at judging results as well as craftsmanship and technique, and as your position holds ten times the responsibility of a writer's and ten times the work, any writer who failed to recognize and abide by your authority would give himself the titles of ingrate and fool.

All of which may be off the subject, but I only wanted you to know that I am so far from repaying any judgment with condemnation that I appreciate a great deal your sacrifice of time ... By the light of this novel I can see to type the next.

Best regards,

L. Ron Hubbard

THE MACAULAY COMPANY

381 FOURTH AVENUE • NEW YORK CITY

July 16th, 1937

Mr. L. Ron Hubbard
Route 1, Box 452
Port Orchard, Washington

Dear Mr. Hubbard:

. . . BUCKSKIN BRIGADES will be published on July 30th. We have already sent six (6) copies to your agent, but I am sending on one copy directly to you by mail.

I presume you will let me see your new manuscripts as they are completed.

In regard to the Great Northern,[1] I am in touch with these people, and as soon as I have some definite word as to what they will do, I will write to you again.

Sincerely yours,

Lee Furman
THE MACAULAY COMPANY

1. Great Northern: the Great Northern Railroad.

LRH and John W. Campbell, Jr.

THE JOHN W. CAMPBELL, JR. LETTERS

No discussion of popular American literature through the 1930s is complete without mention of the frequently brilliant but famously eccentric John W. Campbell, Jr. Readers of *Ron The Writer: The Shaping of Popular Fiction* will recall Mr. Campbell as that techno-minded editor of *Astounding Science Fiction* whom Ron first encountered when summoned to the offices of Street & Smith. Initially, the relationship had been somewhat forced. Street & Smith had ordered Campbell to purchase all LRH submissions as a "humanizing" element to an otherwise inhuman genre and, understandably, Campbell turned bitter. In the end, however, the friendship proved as close as any Campbell would enjoy, and extended well beyond the demise of *Astounding* and Campbell's reign as the undisputed czar of the science fiction realm. Also referenced in letters here is the LRH-Campbell collaboration on the shaping of modern fantasy as initially presented in the pages of *Unknown,* but ultimately reflective in all one finds on the fantasy shelves of bookstores.

SCIENCE-FICTION

79-89 SEVENTH AVENUE, NEW YORK, N. Y

January 23, 1939

Mr. L. Ron Hubbard
Route 1, Box 452
Port Orchard, Wash.

Dear Ron:

I'm damn glad you'll be with us on the Arabian Nights stuff—and you needn't worry about having it yours. I've been telling a few of the boys to read Washington Irving as an example of pure fantasy and complete acceptance of magic, enchantment, et cetera, and adding that they aren't to do Arabian Nights because the field is preempted by you. It's been held open for you.

As soon as I can get hold of a few office copies of UNKNOWN, I'll send one on to you for perusal. "Sinister Barrier," "Trouble With Water" and "Where Angels Fear" are down the alley. "Death Sentence" and "Dark Vision" are pretty fair ideas. The other two are filling space for me acceptably. I'm having a hell of a time with it, because the genuinely first-rate fantasy I demand is hard to get: if it isn't genuinely first-rate, I'm not going to have the magazine I intend to, but just another fantasy magazine.

Basically, this is the philosophy I'm applying: All human beings like wishes to come true. In fairy stories and fantasy, wishes do come true. Adults with childish minds (average "adult" has the mind of a 14 year old) don't dare to read "fairy stories," because their minds are afraid to acknowledge their interest in anything childish—they subconsciously realize their mental immaturity and, as a defense mechanism, avoid childish things.

Your true adult, with fully developed mind, can enjoy fantasy wholeheartedly if it's written in adult words and thought-forms, because, being absolutely confident of his own mental capacity, he doesn't have any sense of embarrassment if caught reading "childish stuff."

You get the same effect in the physical world where you find the big, powerful, capable man pretty generally peaceable, friendly and willing to take ribbing easily because of an assured and unquestionable power. The little runt is apt to be belligerent, spiteful, and bitterly resentful if ribbed.

And every human being likes fantasy fundamentally. All we need is fantasy material expressed in truly adult forms. Every author who honestly and lovingly does that makes a name on it: Lord Dunsany, Washington Irving, Stephen Vincent Benet. In view of this, I have absolute confidence that this new magazine will inevitably become more or less of a fashion among truly adult people—and will be despised by the 14-year-old minds.

I don't, personally, like Westerns particularly, and, in consequence, haven't read your western stuff. But I'm convinced that you do like fantasy, enjoy it, and have a greater gift for fantasy than for almost any other type. The fact that editor after editor has urged you to do that type seems to me indication that you always have had that ability, and that, in avoiding it heretofore, you've suppressed a natural, and not common, talent. There are a lot of boys that turn out readable Westerns, but only about three or four men in a generation that do top-notch fantasy.

And, as I say, I'm reserving the Arabian Nights to you entirely.

Regards,
JOHN W. CAMPBELL, JR.
Editor—UNKNOWN

February 1, 1939

Dear John;

Received your letter and the first copy of UNKNOWN today, for both of which I thank you. I have not yet had a chance to read very deeply but it is very obvious that you have a magazine which ought to sell. The only thing which could possibly kill it would be the tendency common to most writers to try to make the reader <u>believe</u> by disbelieving the thing themselves in the form of the hero's stream of consciousness.

LRH

STREET & SMITH PUBLICATIONS
INCORPORATED
SEVENTY-NINE SEVENTH AVENUE · NEW YORK, N.Y

March 21, 1939

Mr. L. Ron Hubbard,
Route 1, Box 452,
Port Orchard, Wash.

Dear Mr. Hubbard:

The check—largest in UNKNOWN's brief history, and second largest in the combined UNKNOWN-ASTOUNDING history—is on its way. DON'T write more than 45,000 words after this, at least not in one chunk, please.

But, on the other hand, please start now on your next Arabian Nights yarn. What'll it be about? I'd like to get it in about four weeks. If not, then in six weeks. I'm having a hell of a time getting the long stuff, because I consistently and firmly bounce anything below grade B+, and all the novels seem to run about grade C+. And will you tell me when and if you're going to get over your mad at New York and move back where you're convenient? Considering the way the West Coast has treated you, I'd think you'd want to leave it.

You're going to have a sort of competition on Arabian stuff—but of a noncompetitive type, really. Silaki Ali Hassan, full-blooded Arab, is transcribing modern Arabic legends of the Yaffri hill-country[1] for us. They're different in tone from the Baghdad legends of the 1001 Nights.

And—just because UNKNOWN's going, don't forget ASTOUNDING still uses 85,000 words a month. If you must toss off a few shorts between chapters of the novels, how about your strongman from Alpha Centauri who sells the safety pins his father's factory makes?

Forgotten that guy? He sounded like nice material, as I remember it.

Sincerely,
JOHN W. CAMPBELL, JR.
Editor:
UNKNOWN and ASTOUNDING

J. W. Campbell, Jr.

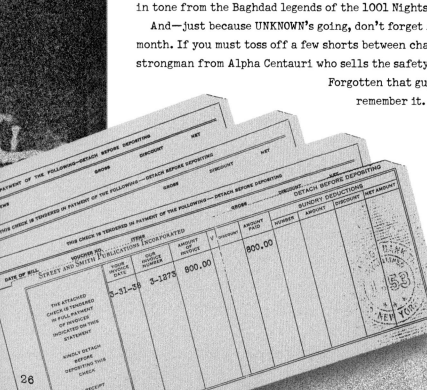

1. Yaffri hill-country: reference to a mountainous region in northern Africa.

April 19, 1939

Mr. L. Ron Hubbard
Route 1, Box 452
Port Orchard, Wash.

Dear Mr. Hubbard:

"Six Stolen Souls" becomes "The Ghoul" and we take it. However, I regret to state that I think it's about B, as against a straight A for your Arabian Nights stuff.

Irish feels forced—Stevie and your little ship-owner-Tiger guy were much more interesting. Also, humor stuff in the fantasy vein is too darned easy to come by; the horror angle is hard to get. This has no horror whatever. The ghoul isn't very menacing, really, because the story is, obviously, straight comedy, and comedy villains are always somewhat inefficient gentlemen.

I've got two long novels on the fire now, so, since you've gotten two successive covers (and something like $1600) I think maybe a novelette or two might be a pious idea. However, if you've got a long novel boiling in your mind, go ahead on that, and maybe for once I'll have a novel for the magazine a few days ahead of when I have to have it.

And may I point out that _my_ telegram was much more stimulating to unknowing telegraph operators than yours? "Six stolen souls stolen or what? Not received. Need thirty to forty thousands. Reply."

You know—white slaving or something on a wholesale scale.

Regards,
JOHN W. CAMPBELL, JR.
Editor

In Defense of the Pulps

Although now acknowledged as a fully vibrant force in popular American literature, the pulps were not infrequently maligned in their day. Charges included stock plots, dull renditions, extraneous violence and unabashed sensationalism—all of which was true, to a point. By the same token, however, those rough-cut and lurid-covered pulps also launched the likes of Dashiell Hammett, Raymond Chandler and many another who would finally prove just as integral to the shaping of American fiction as a Mark Twain or Ernest Hemingway. Then, too, and even more to the point of an L. Ron Hubbard, virtually all we know of modern speculative fiction arguably emerged from the pulps.

Nevertheless, the O. O. McIntyres had their day. A New York critic and political columnist (just to the right of Genghis Khan), McIntyre was typical of those who most condemned the pulps. He resented the sheer size of pulp readership—a full quarter of the American population, and very much including a lesser educated working class. He resented that pervasive sense of heroic defiance woven through so many a grand pulp adventure, e.g., Ron's aforementioned "He Walked to War," telling of a foot-sore Marine fighting for the hell-of-it in a politically irrelevant banana republic. Then again, he almost certainly resented what the top-line pulp author earned; hence, the sly portrayal of the pulpateer as a glorified factory worker.

The LRH reply, actually intended as a letter to the editor, is as accurate as McIntyre is not. That Ron further felt obliged to add, "If you should happen to intimate to a pulpateer that his stories are trash, you are likely to be soundly punched in the nose," would seem to say everything else McIntyre need know about the hard-boiled crew from a great pulp kingdom.

PULPATEER
BY L. RON HUBBARD

A column recently shot across the United States bringing a hitherto unknown side of pulp writing to light. This choice bit of reporting flowed from the pen of the writer's friend, Mr. Odd McIntyre, and to say the very least, it is very odd.

"A weird offshoot of magazine publishing is evidenced in a 'pulp periodical' factory in New York. A company which publishes a string of cheap fiction thrillers has reduced writing to a fine commercial art. Every possible historic plot has been catalogued, and copies are furnished a group of writers who punch the clock like factory hands.

"There are magazines about the West, the sea, the jungles, etc. At the head of the writing staff there is a sort of city editor who apportions each day's work, telling one to write a sea story, using plot Number 4; another a wild west thriller, plot Number 11; and so on.

"Plots of the world's best literature are so twisted that 'Ivanhoe' becomes 'Rutledges Red Revenge.' And the 'Merchant of Venice' becomes 'Love in the Jungle.'

"The men work on salary, like newspapermen, and must turn in so many thousands of words a day. Since the plots are furnished, they only want men who are swift in grinding out copy."

Mr. McIntyre is about due for a new espionage staff. The old one he must control is growing rather rusty, training on crude oil or banana oil or something of the sort. Their reports of late have been growing more and more ludicrous.

Recently, Mr. McIntyre stated that the kingpin of the pulps was making thirty thousand a year, a fact which is very interesting and surprising to the kingpin himself who has had to answer many, many embarrassing questions from various sources to eradicate that statement about Arthur J. Burks.

But never mind, we're thinking about this pulp factory. I have been trying very hard to find out who runs this plant because I would like very much to get into it myself. But evidently Mr. McIntyre has a better source than I have, as I only write for the pulps for a living.

My information must be very limited. In fact I have not written for anybody but the Big Five and the little five and a few others. Dell, Standard, Street & Smith, Munsey, and last but not least: Popular, have seen fit at one time and another to print my stories in any and all lengths covering every angle of the pulp field but the love story. Other, lesser firms have done the same.

Now I am very angry about all this because it seems to me that some of my companies must have been holding out on me. I think that I ought to rate being on a staff which writes to Plot Number 4, 6, or maybe 9. That would be so simple, you see, and I would never have to worry about things like rent and hospital bills and new shoes for the kids. Somebody is obviously holding out on me.

But all foolish remarks to the contrary, I wish all these columnists, in their lofty heights of literarity, would stick to their last. There has been another one of these pulp-attack epidemics going the rounds and it seems to be catching. THE AMERICAN MERCURY published a very good article on the subject which was rather true and fair but altogether too bitter.

Red Propaganda Is On Increase

By O. O. McINTYRE

EVERY worker in the writing trade knows there is an increasing and subtle spread of Communistic propaganda in New York by men and women who follow the same calling. Sly pinks who howl their denials when accused! A number of them have been referred to with illuminating citations in exposures by "The Red Net Work."

O. O. McINTYRE

However, few patriotic scribblers resenting such under-cover methods and despising their treasonable nature have done anything about it. H. L. Mencken is about the only one to speak out. It has become smart in New York's writing circle to sneer at the Constitution and intimate Jefferson and some of the other bulwarks of Democracy were mossbacks with theories outgrown. The complaisance of those loyal to American ideals is astonishing.

Some day, I think, many may regret this indifference. Just now the so-called literati seems sickly pale with white corpuscles.

Especially in the more sophisticated publications and novels are the hoots between the lines for cherished ideals growing more insolent.

Two books—and I won't give them a free puff by mentioning titles—during the month intimate that the Moscow life is the real existence and that capitalistic America is for morons. Yet for "cover up" purposes there are passages that would make prosecution for sedition difficult. It is trick writing to escape any possible stigma. But the poison of social discontent is there.

I have sickened of literary teas because of the Van Dyked boys with third-rate professorships who get their crowd in the corner and spew insinuations in the guise of good, clean fun.

They do not need a bawling out. They need a few socks in the jaw, which they would receive in similar gatherings in, say, Texas, Montana or Arizona. Here they have amiable "yessers" who fear they will be thought extremely backwoods not to concur that Socialistic and Marxian doctrines are hot stuff.

The greatest statesman in the history of France, after civilization had been uprooted and human blood ran in torrents, wrote a letter to his son saying: "Our indifference brought us here!"

* * *

A weird offshoot of magazine publishing is evidenced in a "pulp periodical" factory in New York. A company which publishes a string of cheap fiction thrillers has reduced writing to a fine commercial art. Every possible historic plot has been catalogued, and copies are furnished a group of writers who punch the clock like factory hands.

There are magazines about the West, the sea, the jungles, etc. At the head of the writing staff is a sort of city editor who apportions each day's work, telling one to write a sea story, using plot No. 4; another a Wild West thriller, plot No. 11; and so on.

Plots of world's best in literature are so twisted that "Ivanhoe" becomes "Rutledge's Red Revenge," and "The Merchant of Venice" becomes "Love in the Jungle."

The men work on salary, like newspapermen, and must turn in so many thousands of words a day. Since the plots are furnished, they only want men who are swift in grinding out copy.

* * *

Fashion secret: A milliner tells me that small hats for women are dictated by their convenience in getting in and out of motor cars.

* * *

True picture yarn: A fellow wrote a magazine story. A picture company bought and paid for it. The author spent the money. Three weeks later the same picture company called up the same author about the same story.

These things do a pulpateer no little harm. Primarily, a pulpateer is a very decent writer (he has to be that, you know). He is sincere about his work as any of the top rankers will testify. If you should happen to intimate to a pulpateer that his stories are trash, you are likely to be soundly punched in the nose—and rightly. He tries to write his very best and make his stories exciting and often he gets a lot more than excitement into them.

There is no real reason for ignorant people to rip and tear at a man's livelihood and vocation and avocation when it actually means nothing to said people. Such backhanded slaps hurt not a little. The idea that pulp writing is mechanical is already too prevalent.

Here is what such a thing does: A friend of mine, earning his bread by adding figures or fixing streetcars or flying transport planes reads such an article or statement. He does not bother to acquaint himself with the facts any more than the man who wrote the remark did. Instantly, however, this friend of mine says, "So that's what Hubbard is doing. Hell, I thought he was a real writer."

And the next time I see the man he is apt to make some jest concerning my work and he is no longer a friend of mine.

These things put a bar between a pulpateer and the writing world, a bar which really should not exist. In articles, for instance, I often have to interview prominent men in this field and that. In stories I sometimes feel that my information is not quite sound. To give everyone an even break I look up someone who is directly connected with my subject. In explaining myself I say that this will be for "War Birds" or "Adventure" and if he is a reader

of magazines in the so-called quality group, or of columns, he is apt to smile at me and tell me, "No thanks, I don't want to appear in such cheap magazines."

That has happened to me before and it will happen again. How can I do a sincere and honest job, for instance, with the Coast Guard under such conditions? And yet the story or article will be read by a hundred thousand or more people who are rather impressionable. If I'm wrong, they get the Coast Guard wrong and then there's a double howl about it.

Outside of losing my friends, demeaning my profession and undermining my sources, the sales of such magazines may be hurt as a consequence. People (although I'm sure I don't know why) believe what they read in the papers.

Such remarks discourage pulp tyros and keep them from a possible living by causing them to write down to their markets.

In the case of the old dime novel (which Odd McIntyre probably read and enjoyed in his true "homey" style as a kid) it has recently been discovered that the finest sources of Western America as it was lay in these same paper-covered books. The men who wrote those stories were, for the most part, former punchers, sailors, soldiers of fortune and God knows what else. In, for instance, "Colonel Prentiss Ingraham's"[1] LAFITTE'S LIEUTENANT, in his BRAND OF THE RED ANCHOR, I have found a startling knowledge of historical types of vessels, of gunnery, tactics, and costume. I had recourse to such sources while I was writing one called UNDER THE BLACK ENSIGN and I checked Ingraham and found he knew a lot more than I did for all my study.

The dime novel, booed in its day, is now filed carefully in the rare book collection of the Library of Congress.

A surprising number of historical novels, well reviewed when they came out in book form, have appeared serially in pulps. A large number of pulp stories are now carefully bound up in anthologies.

To defame the pulps and the pulpateer seems to be a habit with so-called quality writers, columnists, and novelists. They are in another quite different strata. They talk about something indefinite which they call art and then they sit down to their typewriters and dash out something they read with ecstasy but which may be so faulty that an honest author cringes. Witness, for God's sake, MAN ON THE FLYING TRAPEZE, and then glance through the as yet serial ONE WOMAN ALIVE which takes as its source what a lot of us have been doing for years under the name of pseudo-scientific. More originality has appeared in WEIRD TALES per story than H. G. Wells put into THINGS TO COME.

I could name you scores of famous authors who trained in pulp. Their training must have been sound because their works are sound. Only one detective writer who is now famous scorns the pulps. He never appeared on wood-pulp paper and never tried to read it over. He had the popular touch and he got it second hand from writers who served their 'prenticeship in pulp.

It amuses me to read in McIntyre's column about this man and that, evidently very revered by McIntyre, and then to remember that this man came up through rough paper.

To glance over the pulps on the stands you cannot help but

1. Colonel Prentiss Ingraham: as a scout who traveled in the company of Buffalo Bill, he wrote stories recounting adventures on the American frontier.

31

Mystery!

ing Novel

FEATURE
NOVEL
by L. Ron
Hubbard
author of
"Sabotage in Town"

Death
At
Sund

Don't Rush Me

DON'T RUSH ME

By L. RON HUBBARD

The trench was never dug—
yet Sergeant Marshall had to
hold it from the enemy!

THERE is a superstition among military men that coveted stripes are won through carrying out orders to the letter and file number, that all details must be effected with neatness and despatch, that recognition is gained only through close attention to duty.

But take the case of Daniel Reyburn Marshall, sergeant to Company H in the town of San Pedro during the last unpleasantness in Nicaragua. Marshall was sergeant because the Marine Corps couldn't afford to withhold his stripes. He knew more tactics than his shavetail and more theory than the

Sabres flashed in the light of the burning garrison.

ILLUSTRATED BY FRANK VOLP

26

DANGER IN THE DARK

—bases a story on the authentic legend of
vast Todamona—the shark-god of the islands.

L. Ron Hubbard

BILLY NEWMAN looked wearily at the apathetic face and needed no fine physician to tell him that he gazed upon death.

The DIVE

Had Lucky Martin, the famous test pilot, escaped death in the
air only to fall into the steel trap of a foreign power's maneuvers
in the arms race?

remark the names on the covers. If you know anything about pulp you can doubtlessly recall little bits of this and that man's history.

Pulpateers, columns to the contrary, are an assorted, romantic crew, making their livings with their typewriters and doing very well at it. Right here I really ought to prove this by citing a few cases, but the mere thought makes me recoil. I don't want this to be a book, but an article. These men and women have done everything and anything you can name. Reporters, punchers, detectives, wanderers, professors, sergeants, captains, columnists (beg pardon, Odd), sailors, movie writers, salesmen, city editors, and so on and on and on. One chap I enjoy reading is, to my surprise, a full-fledged general. Another (three in fact) is a Commander of the Legion of Honor. Another has been decorated by two kings. Still another has jumped the ocean twice. One was city ed[itor] for an NY daily (his hobby was firing columnists). Another is a civil engineer with years in the tropics to his credit. Another commanded a Turkish division in the World War. Another is a World War ace. But, as I said, I could go on forever.

Now in thinking all this over, doesn't it seem to you that a man who can only mark one track (from his home town to the darkness of a New York apartment) down on his personal map rather sticks his neck into the guillotine when he passes judgment on the work of men, not mice?

There isn't any real reason for such idiotic and erroneous statements which are made without the least effort at verification.

The trouble with these critics seems to be that they stamp out on ground they have never seen.

I venture to say that these critics have never seen a pulp magazine anywhere but on a newsstand. Perhaps it would be educational if they would buy a copy of a pulp and sit themselves down to read it.

There are rotten stories in the pulps, of course, but with great candor I can verify the statement that there are lousy stories in the slicks, in books, and in the little magazines. We do not condemn these three fields in one lump remark. I don't get the point of lumping all pulps and all pulp stories into one great class.

And I don't get the point in running down men who are trying to do a job as well as they can.

As for having Plot 4 and Plot 11 furnished, McIntyre might be a wiser man if he tried to write and sell a pulp story. I doubt that he could. I know dozens of people who are always sidling up to a writer and saying, "I've got a swell plot for you." The plot, I might say, is a very small part of a story. Handling is a fine art and handling determines the yarn from beginning to end.

Please pardon me when I smile a little at Mr. McIntyre's selection of plot sources. "Ivanhoe," according to [Sir Walter] Scott's own statement, is a pulp yarn. The plot of the "Merchant of Venice" had been used several thousand times before Shakespeare ever plagiarized it. You can find both plots in Greek, and in Arabic.

Plot, Mr. McIntyre, is the least of a pulpateer's worries. I have an agent who drowns me in plots I cannot use. I was once given a book which contains millions of plots and I cannot use that either. I recently saw a pack of cards which dealt of plot but, although they might help somebody they don't help me.

During the past year I sold many hundreds of thousands of words, and I don't happen to be ashamed of any story in the lot. In fact, Mr. McIntyre, I would like to forward you the file for your education. I once gave a college short story professor a twenty thousand worder to read. He had never read a pulp story in his life and yet he was eager to heap sarcasm upon my head. He read this story all right, and it kept him up until dawn. He has had nothing to say about pulp since. Maybe the dose would be good for you, too.

When I look for tripe to read, I don't go to the pulps. I go to the magazine section of the Sunday papers. I think pulpateers avoid that market because the pay is too small and too irregular.

And here is one last, parting shot. I have a few slick paper friends and I've loaned most of them money at one time or another. I don't want anything to do with slick paper . . . I couldn't write light love and the old trite doctor-in-love plot anyway because it is too bare.

But just by way of proving that pulpateers aren't really machines, I have a couple books on the way up. I'll forward some copies to you. I might as well do something with the books because they certainly won't make over a cent a word even if they happen to become bestsellers.

This is a mild protest, I assure you. If at any time you wish to know anything, Mr. McIntyre, about writing and writers, please communicate with some writers for a change.

###

DEAR SIR, WOULD YOU TELL ME HOW TO WRITE?

Among other comments regularly heard in reference to the L. Ron Hubbard of 1935: He possessed a singularly rare concern for those who wished to write but lacked both editorial direction and contacts. He worked ceaselessly to open traditionally bolted doors of reputable agents and publishers, and otherwise stood ready to help all those who harbored the dream of writing for a living. The statements are true, as the letters to follow will attest.

Regarding those letters: While publishers were theoretically open to all submissions, senior editors generally reviewed only those manuscripts of known authors or those offered through agents whom they likewise knew. The catch: one could not enlist an agent unless previously published, or at least recommended by an author of repute. In reply, and especially in his capacity as president of American Fiction Guild's New York chapter, LRH fought to admit the unpublished author as a "novice." Whereupon, he would usher them into the rear of Rostoff's Restaurant for those all-important introductions to editors and publishers lunching on club sandwiches.

Offered here is a sampling of the to-and-from novice authors, including an obscure Catherine L. Moore—then employed as a bank secretary, but latterly remembered for a long and distinguished career as a novelist and teleplay writer. Additionally included are Ron's "solid meat" replies to the "word-weary," and his letter from the airwaves of Radio KVOO—all in answer to that question of questions: "Would you tell me how to write?"

Dear Mr. Hubbard;

For a long time I have been writing fiction. Most of it came back and lies neglected in my files along with letters from editors and plain rejects.

I have not managed to sell a single line. Of course I had some published in the school paper and a few places like that but I think that if I could get at it right I could earn a good living by writing.

The man down at the service station has read a lot of my stories and has given me quite a lot of good advice on them. He took a writing course, I think, or maybe it was journalism, at the local university.

Is it asking too much for you to answer this question? How did you start to write and sell?

Respectfully,
Jim Higgins

Dear Higgins;

It isn't a question of how I started to write, it's a question of why.

There's a world of difference there. I take it that you have a job, otherwise you wouldn't eat and if you don't eat, you don't last long.

We assume, therefore, that you are eating. That is bad, very bad. No man who wants to start writing should be able to eat regularly. Steaks and potatoes get him out of trim.

When a man starts to write, his mental attitude should be one of anguish. He has to sell something because he has to pay the grocery bill.

My advice to you is simple. If you have the idea that you can write saleable stuff, go off someplace and get short of money. You'll write it all right, and what's more you'll sell it.

Witness the case of a lady I know in New York. She was plugging at writing for some fifteen years without selling a line. She left the Big Town with her husband. In the Pacific Northwest her husband died and left her stranded.

She went to work in a lumber mill and wrote a book about it and sold it first crack out. She worked as a waitress and wrote a book about that and sold it.

Having succeeded with two books, she went back to the Big Town and got herself a job in the library until the returns came in. She wrote all the time after that but she was eating. In sawmill and hash house she wasn't living comfortably. She needed the extra.

She hasn't sold a line since.

The poet in the garret is not a bad example, after all. Personally I write to pay my bills.

Jack London, I am told, plastered his bills over his writing desk and every time he wanted to get up or go arty he glanced at them and went right on grinding it out.

I think if I inherited a million tomorrow my stuff would go esoteric and otherwise blah.

I started to write because I had come back from the West Indies where I had been hunting gold and discovered that we had a depression going on up here. . . . I had to start eating right away.

I started writing one story a day for six weeks. I wrote that story in the afternoon and evening. I read the mag I was to make the next day before I went to bed. I plotted the yarn in my sleep, rose and wrote it, read another mag all the way through, went to bed. . . .

Out of that month and a half of work I have sold fiction to the sum of nine hundred dollars. At the end of the six weeks I received checks amounting to three hundred and two dollars and fifty cents.

Unable to stand prosperity I left for California. I got broke there, wrote for a month without stopping to breathe, sold eleven hundred dollars worth.

Nothing like necessity to take all this nonsense about how you ought to reform editors right out of your head.

As far as that guy down at the service station is concerned, he may be okay, but remember this: You are the writer. You have to learn your own game. And if he's never hit the bread and butter side of the business, he knows less about it than you do, all courses to the contrary.

Write me again when you've gone and done some tall starving.

Best regards,

L. Ron Hubbard

Dear Mr. Hubbard;
    I have always felt that I could write if I tried, but somehow I've been so busy during the last few years that I haven't had much chance.
    I was married when I was very young and every time I started my writing, Joe would either move (Joe is my husband) or we'd have to both work because of the bills.
    Most of my children have grown up now to a point where they can take care of themselves and although I have some time now I don't seem to be able to get down to work. I have a lot of stories in the back of my head but I just can't find time or ways and means of getting them down on paper. I feel that this is mostly mental.
    Would you tell me how you write?

Wishfully,
Mary Stein

Dear Mary Stein;
    Remember when you read this that I didn't ask to be appointed your psycho-analyst. I am nothing but a hard-working writer, after all, using fictitious characters and working them over. When real people get planted in front of me I stand back and gape and wonder if it can be true.
    Let me tell you about Margaret Sutton. She writes some of the best children's books being written today. She has five kids, I think. A lot of them need plenty of attention. She has to support them and do her own work and everything.
    One day somebody asked her why she didn't get a maid now she had so much royalty money. She blinked and said, "A maid? Why, what would I do with my extra time?"
    Well, there you have it. Maybe it _is_ mental.
    From Crabtown to Timbuktu, when I have been introduced as a writer, somebody always has said, "Well, now, I could write too if I just had some time."
    That is a queer mental quirk with people. If a man is a writer, he is doing something everybody thinks they can do. A chap who is the head of a big insurance company, highly successful, once said to me, "I would like to write, but I never seem to be able to find the time."
    It's their way of apology, I guess. Nearly everyone makes that remark and, to be brutally frank, it is a source of much merriment in the professional ranks.
    I am not one to talk about working and writing in the same breath. I have a law around the house here which says that writing comes first and to hell with everything else. The lawn grows into an alfalfa field, the pipes drip merrily, the floors need paint, but I turn a deaf ear to pleas and go right on writing.
    I have found this to be the case. My time at the typewriter is worth, per hour, what the average artisan gets per week. I do not work the same hours he does. I work far less, but I work much harder.
    Therefore I paint my floors and fix my pipes with the typewriter keys, if you get me. One short story will pay for all the work to be done around this house in a month including the maid's wages.
    People let petty things keep them away from a typewriter. I think that is true because they _want_ to be kept away from the machine. When you start to write there seems to be an invisible wall separating you from the keyboard. Practice is the only thing which will dissipate it.
    If you make yourself write during trying times, you are doing a lot toward whipping your jinx.
    Recently I was very ill in a New York apartment. My agent, Ed Bodin, and his wife came in. . . .
    They left at 8:45 P.M. They returned at 11:30. In the interim I had grown restless. I felt that I was stale, would be unable to write anything for months. Then I got mad at such a traitorous thought, climbed out of bed, sat down at the mill and wrote a story which I gave to Ed upon his return.
    I knew, of course, that the story would be rotten. Half the time I couldn't see the paper, I was so dizzy.
    But I guess I was wrong. Ed sold it almost immediately to DETECTIVE FICTION WEEKLY. It was "The Mad Dog Murders."
My contention is that, if you have the stuff on the ball, you can write anytime, anyplace and anything.

Best regards,

L. Ron Hubbard

Dear Mr. Hubbard;

I been pounding out a lot of Western yarns and shipping same to certain editors located in New York, where the only horse in town is located on a whisky bottle.

These gents claim, per letter and returned stories, that I haven't got any real feel of the West.

The same irritates me considerable. I spotted a yarn of yours and you seemed to know hosses hands down and guns likewise and that don't measure like most of these Western yarns.

I think maybe I better go back to wranglin' hosses because maybe I don't know how to put it in stories, I sure do know something about putting them in corrals.

I thought it was about time somebody wrote some Western stories that knew what they was writing about. I still think so.

The question is, what the hell can I do about it?

Yours truly,
Steed Monahan

Dear Steed Monahan;

You have laid the finger on something. I'm not sure what. I wouldn't go as far as to say that you have the dope but lack the knack of writing fiction. You know there might be something in that. Anyway, I'm no judge because I never read any of your stuff.

This question once leaped up at a New York Chapter meeting of the American Fiction Guild. Clee Woods, Al Echols, Sayer, and maybe Tom Roan got pretty deep into the argument about whether or not you had to know the West to write Westerns.

I wasn't so very interested because my forte is adventure and such, but I listened because I had been raised in Montana but had never been able to sell a good Western story.

These lads who knew the West had it all settled to their satisfaction that you had to have the dope and data before you could put down the words and syllables.

Then Frank Gruber stood up and said he'd sold a few Westerns that year. Fifteen or so. And that was odd because, he said, he had never been closer to a ranch than editing a chicken paper[1] in the Middle West.

So there you are. The dope and data does not outweigh good story writing. I can write stories about pursuit pilots, stories about coal miners, stories about detectives, stories about public enemies, G-men, arctic explorers, Chinese generals, etc.

Which doesn't mean that I had to shoot down another plane to get the dope. I have never: 1. Been in a coal mine. 2. Been a detective. 3. A public enemy. 4. Been a G-man. 5. Explored the Arctic. 6. Been a Chinese general.

And yet I am proud of a record which was only marred by one inaccuracy in a story, and that very trivial. By getting experience somewhere near the field, I can exploit the field.

For instance, of late, I have been looking into dangerous professions. I've climbed skyscrapers with steeplejacks, dived with deep-sea divers, stunted with test pilots, and made faces at lions. But at no time was I actually a member of that particular profession of which I was to write. I didn't have to be because the research enabled me to view it from a longer, more accurate range.

The only thing you can do is try hard to write a swell, fast action Western yarn. Peddle it to every Western book in the field. Ask for some honest comments on it.

But before you do this, be sure you are writing what these magazines are buying.

A good story comes first. Information comes second. An editor of one of our best books recently told me, "Accuracy be damned. Very few gentlemen will know you're wrong. Give us the story. We can buy the accuracy from a twenty-five a week clerk with a library card. You don't have to <u>know</u>. You can <u>write</u>."

Ride 'em, cowboy, and don't pull any leather[2] until they spot your trouble for you. But if you can't write, you can't write, no matter how much you know.

And I guess that's all I know about that subject.

Best regards,

L. Ron Hubbard

1. chicken paper: a journal of poultry farming.
2. pull any leather: a rider of a bucking horse in a rodeo is not allowed to "pull leather," i.e., to grab the saddle horn (of leather) to steady himself.

Dear Mr. Hubbard;

   During the last few months I have managed to sell some of my stories to magazines located in New York. I have every assurance that I can keep right on selling these stories of mine and I think it's about time I made a break for the Big Town.

   I've been reading the writer's magazines and I think you have to know all about New York and the markets before you can really get places in this game.

   I've been making over a hundred dollars a month in the writing game . . . I asked one of the editors about this and he told me by all means look him up when I got to New York. As that sounds encouraging, I'm planning on leaving.

   Jeb wants me to go with him to Baffin Land on his whaler this summer, but I think I better give my writing a break and go to New York instead.

   But I thought, before I made a decision, I'd better write to some professional writer like you who's been in New York a lot and ask him what conditions were there.

   My stories are mostly about this part of the world as I am always cruising around or trekking off someplace with guys like Jeb, or Carlson (he's the Mounty here), but I think I ought to have a wider field for my work. Detective stories, for instance and things like that.

   Would you tell me about New York?

Sincerely,
Arch Bankey

Dear Arch Bankey;

A few years ago I knew a beachcomber in Hong Kong. All he ever talked about was the day he would go to New York. That was the place. New York!

But he was smarter than the rest of us. He never went. He just talked about it.

There's nothing like knowing your editors, of course. Editors are swell people as a rule. Nothing like getting their slant face to face. Increase your sales no end.

But if you think you can go to New York and live there on a hundred a month, you're as crazy as a locoed wolf. Think about it from this angle:

In New York you'll have noise, bad living conditions, and higher expenses. You will have to keep right on writing to keep eating.

You are used to writing where the biggest noise is a pine tree shouting at its neighbor. That is the condition you know. You can write there.

Chances are a hundred to one that you won't be able to turn out a line when the subway begins to saw into your nerves, when the L[1] smashes out your eardrums overhead, when ten thousand taxi drivers clamp down on their horns.

If you can't write, you can't eat because you won't have enough reserve.

Besides, the markets you mention are not very reliable. Those eds are the brand that wants something for nothing. Wait until you sell the big books in the pulp field. Wait until you crack into at least four of the big five publishing houses. Wait until you are pretty sure you know what you're doing in the game before you make a change.

I've wrecked myself time after time with changes just because I have itchy feet. I have just come from New York. I got along all right, for a very little while, then the town got me. I had a big month and managed to get out.

But once New York gets you, you're got.

Some of the swellest guys I know are in New York. Also some of the worst heels.

Here's my advice, take it for what it's worth to you.

Jeb and the whaler will provide you with lots of story material. Go with him and write it. Trek out with that Mounty and study the way he goes about it. Take your trips with your eyes open for data.

Neither Jeb nor Carlson will let you starve. If you can't put out the wordage, you'll find editors far from interested in you.

Write everything you can, study the mags you're sending stuff to, collect every scrap of story material. Collect yourself checks to the amount of one thousand dollars no more no less. With that all in one piece, shove off for New York.

On arrival get yourself the best clothes you can buy. Register at the Waldorf-Astoria. Take editors out to lunch in a Cadillac taxi.

Stay in New York until all you've got left is your return trip ticket. Pack up and leave right away quick for home.

Don't try to work in New York. Don't try to make it your home. Go there with a roll and do the place right, then grab the rattler for Hudson Bay before the glamour wears off.

Sitting in a shabby room, pounding a mill with the landlady pounding on the door is fine experience, but I think gunning for whales up off Baffin Land is much more to your liking.

Best regards,

L. Ron Hubbard

---

1. L: short for elevated railway system.

170 King Street
North Bay, Ontario
29th May 1936

Mr. L. Ron Hubbard
40 King Street
New York City, NY

Dear Mr. Hubbard,

  Received your very generous letter in answer to my query.
I feel I cannot let it pass without letting you know how much I
appreciate the trouble you took to inform me about things I
couldn't have known otherwise, or without wasting a good deal
of time, effort and perhaps money. A three-page letter packed
full of meat of the kind I've been wanting is what I got.
Thanks to you, I am going at the writing game much less blindly
with regard to trying to hit markets, and with a good deal more
confidence. To show you there IS a great disadvantage in being
away from the hub of things, it's taken me nearly four years of
blind groping to get the sort of stuff you've handed me from
your experience as a writer that has arrived. I'm not likely to
forget you took the trouble to grind out three pages of that
experience, when honestly I expected a terse reply, if any at
all. And that cynical attitude is largely the result of
accumulated rejection slips, which in turn, in many cases were
the result of not knowing the ropes.

                    Yours sincerely,
                    Gordon Walsh

June 15, 1937

Dear Mr. Hubbard:

I suppose you're wondering of all things, how in the dickens did I ever get hold of your address. Well, it's all pretty simple, when you stop to figure it out. The fact of the matter is, I had occasion to drop in on Ed Bodin, your agent. Naturally, we drifted into conversation. Fell to talking of things pretty general, when all of a sudden: "What's become of Ron Hubbard?" I said. Just like that. I wish you could have seen his face. "Ron Hubbard?" he smiled back at me. "Why, haven't you heard? Hubbard's out in Hollywood." I stared at him a moment in surprise. "Out in Hollywood!" I exclaimed. "This is the first time I've heard of that." "Why, sure," he went on. "Hubbard's got a ten-week contract with the COLUMBIA PICTURE people. He's doing the continuity of a serial for them."

And that's that! Boy, am I glad! Truthfully, if you were my own brother—my own flesh and blood—I couldn't feel more elated. You know how some things just naturally give one a great big thrill? Well, that's just the way this joyful news affected me. "Why the hero worship," you say? Oh, this hero worship of mine—if you may choose to call it such—isn't so hard to explain, Mr. Hubbard. It's founded upon some pretty good substantial reasons. One mighty good reason I might mention right offhand is that I enjoy your stories. You're a dandy good writer. You can be depended upon to turn out interesting story material.

However, it isn't because of this one fact alone—that I enjoy your stories—that I have such a great feeling of admiration and liking for you. There is something else. This something I speak of, has more to do with you as an—INDIVIDUAL. It is a something I believe to be inherent in your nature. Do you know what this something is? It's your—HUMANNESS. Here's where you shine, Ron Hubbard. You delight in giving the other fellow a lift up. A little better realization and understanding of the pure joy of living. How do I know? Why, I've experienced it. Do you think I've forgotten how kind you were to me at some of those WRITER'S GUILD meetings? I must have bored you to death. However, this didn't faze you; not one iota. There you were, listening to me with all the tolerance and sympathy in the world...More power to YOU! How can a fellow do otherwise than wish such a man as YOU success in any new venture.

Frankly, my one sincere hope is that they sign you up in this picture game at an enormous salary for the rest of your whole natural life...

                    Very Sincerely Yours,
                    James F. Ayres

                    St. Francis Hotel
                    5533 Hollywood Blvd.
                    Hollywood, Calif.
                    June 28, 1937

Dear Ayres;

Your letter was quite a pleasing surprise. I have been wondering what markets you were hitting by this time.

You give me very sparse data about yourself. Are you rolling them steadily? And if so, for whom? Pardon my ignorance but I haven't had time to even look at a magazine for months.

You wish me a most horrible fate in your last line. I'll be very happy to get out of this town. A good pulpateer can make more money in his own markets with the same amount of work. That sounds odd, but then I never work fourteen hours a day on my own stories. Seven days a week. It's more like four hours a day four days a week.

I have finished my original job and now I'm waiting for a report and filling in the time turning out some other stories and getting them into the studios. In addition to this work I have managed to write several novelettes in the past six weeks and as a consequence my energy is at a very low ebb.

Art Burks and George Bruce are out here but I see very little of Bruce. Art and I get together two or three times a week and swear at the movies.

Here's wishing you lots of sales.

                    Best regards,

                    L. Ron Hubbard

Catherine Moore
2547 Brookside Parkway,
South Drive
Indianapolis, Indiana
July 14, 1937

Dear Ron Hubbard:

If it really were an ivory tower in which your letter reached me I'd probably have answered it much sooner. It's been more like an ivory madhouse since my return from California, and though I've been home two weeks I'm not entirely unpacked even yet, which should give you some idea.

Were you in Hollywood at the same time I was? And one of the many interesting people Forrest[1] told me I was missing by leaving for San Francisco so soon? If so I'm awfully disappointed and can only look forward to next fall and your possible trip East, which I hope nothing interferes with. The nice lady of the secondhand magazine shop has written me since you did, sketching a personality that I certainly don't want to miss—one to match your hair, she implies.

I bought FIVE NOVELS several days ago, and last night finally succeeded in finding time to read your "Dive Bomber"—which, I noted with vicarious pride, had first place in the magazine. And I'm pleased and flattered, but not convinced, by the suggestion that our writing is similar. Your taste is so much better than mine. I mean, your very vivid and colorful descriptions come in small doses, instead of encrusting the story so thickly that one's slightly sick from the richness by the time the tale's finished. My stories are like making a meal off chocolate pie and plum pudding, while yours have a sufficient admixture of rare beef-steak and beer and salad to make the dessert welcome instead of cloying.

I think I've come to a crossroads so far as my fantastic writing is concerned. Looking back, I itch for a blue pencil. So much of it would be so much better if a lot of the rococo were cut out. I write in iambic pentameter, for one thing, and too much prose poetry is too much. You've got a feeling of sustained rhythm in your own writing which happily stops short of the sing-song, as mine so often and so unfortunately doesn't. When I have evolved through morasses of over-writing and wordiness and rococo into something approaching what I want to be like, I think the finished product will be very like your own style. Restrained and succinct, yet capable of brief and vivid descriptions all the more vivid for their brevity. Like a couple of lines in a poem I'm fond of, describing a Japanese print, "The skill to do more—With the will to refrain."

Your advice about breaking into other markets than fantasy is one I'm trying to follow, so far without success. I have so little time to write, and so many things to be done in that spare time after working hours, and I'm so lazy anyhow, that somehow I don't seem to

1. Forrest: Forrest Ackerman, science fiction editor and agent.

get much done. Otis Kline is tutoring me, and with his help maybe the day will come when I can expand a bit in my markets. Meanwhile your encouragement helps a lot. With your experience you should know what you're talking about, and I'm extremely flattered and pleased.

Do you really like writing for a living? You must have bad times when you can't write anything. Doesn't it scare you? Or perhaps you have a separate income. Of course it's a comfort to have a steady job such as mine, with salary coming in whether my mind's a blank or not, but I certainly haven't much time to write. What I need, of course, is someone to stand over me with a long whip to raise a welt on me every time the typewriter lags.

Well, I've a passionate longing to visit Sweden—can't imagine why—so maybe that will prove an incentive. Anyhow, I'll keep your letter and read it over at low ebbs for encouragement.

I am much awed by the fact that you were writing a movie. Was it your first? Why did you have to go to Hollywood to do it? How'd you get the chance? And how badly do you expect to get gypped? I've always heard that unless you're someone like—Oh, Wodehouse or Galsworthy or somebody—you could just expect to be wretchedly underpaid and miserably treated and brazenly pirated if you write for the movies. I have an aunt and an uncle both of whom did a bit of scenario writing years ago, with all the above results. But maybe the Hollywood morals have improved since. Reading over the above, I realize it's somewhat on the order of the famous—"So the wolf left Little Red Riding Hood lying in a pool of blood, torn limb from limb . . . good ni-i-ight kiddies, sweet dreams!" I didn't really mean to paint the picture in such horrid colors, and doubtless you know much more about it than I do. I hope you can dispel my nightmarish impressions and tell me that all is sweetness and light at Columbia Pictures.

I'm on the lookout for BUCKSKIN BRIGADES, which sounds very pleasant. It's going to be fun reading more of your work—I like it very much indeed.

Have you an agent? And what do you really want to do—write novels, or for the movies, or for the slicks, or what? How do you intend to go about working toward the desired end? I wouldn't hesitate to ask questions for fear of being thought inquisitive, of course. You seem to be at the place I hope to reach in a few years—writing widely for the pulps, with a book or two out, beginning to cast glances into the greener pastures beyond. And any technical advice you can give me will be deeply appreciated. . . .

Anyhow, thanks a great deal for all the encouragement, and for liking my gilded-gingerbread style of writing.[2]

Gratefully,
Catherine Moore

2. Although an extended search reveals no further LRH-Moore correspondence, we know their friendship had been lengthy--moreover, and notwithstanding her "gilded-gingerbread style," Ms. Moore went on to enjoy a profitable career as both an author of science fiction and a regular contributor to the 1960s hit television series, 77 Sunset Strip.

KVOO

PHILTOWER · TULSA

February 21, 1938

Mr. L. Ron Hubbard
Western Story Magazine
Street & Smith, Inc.
New York, N.Y.

Dear Mr. Hubbard,

Thursdays at 10:00 P.M., Central Time, I am doing a program called "Writers and Readers" in which is a department called "The Story Behind The Story." Would you send me the "inside" of one of your stories? Notes on the birth of the idea, speed or slowness of sale, technical notes. What any writer wonders about the other guy's story. If you will send me publication date, I'll match the broadcast date and make it a tie-up. We can be heard all over the country at night.

My aim is to publicize the pulps and their writers, and, if even in a small way, make the field greener for us who are feeding in it.

Whatever biographical notes you send with the above will be used.

Cordially,

Bob De Haven

Announcer

KVOO
Bob De Haven
March 10, 1938

Writers and Readers

Good evening, writers and readers, this is Bob De Haven with the Writers and Readers program. What is it? Well, a chat about the great game of putting words into print for entertainment and a chat of interest to those behind as well as in front of the magazines, books and pictures.

Tonight we have the story behind the story contributed by L. Ron Hubbard . . . who writes from the Knickerbocker Hotel in New York. Heaven only knows where he is now. First I'll get you acquainted with Hubbard before going into his story which is on the stands now in Street & Smith's <u>Western Story</u> magazine.

Hubbard was born in Nebraska and moved to Oklahoma at the age of three weeks, moved in with his grandfather, Lafe Waterbury, who had an outfit near Durant. Eventually he went to Montana where the war took his father away in the navy and L. Ron spent years tagging his father around the world.

With his father and independently, L. Ron Hubbard had traveled a quarter of a million at nineteen years through Asia, South Pacific and South America. He then stopped trying to be a civil engineer and tried to be a pilot. He searched for gold in Latin America, ran an expedition and started to write while trailing around the globe. He has sold one of every type of story printed. His published word total is about a million and a half.

His last book was called *Buckskin Brigades* . . .

So with that introduction let's turn to his story behind the story. It has been on the stands this past week in *Western Story* magazines, the lead story called "Six-Gun Caballero." It was written several months ago and he says the details are hard to recall because a story written, to him, exists as an individual piece of work and he can't remember a time when it was not written. But he does recall every move that his principal character, Michael Patrick Obanon made in "Six-Gun Caballero." He came alive before the story started through the typewriter. Hubbard would know him anywhere.

This sounds like characters haunt him and that's right. One character haunted him for four and a half years and made his life miserable. In truth, he *was* a ghost, this character. He was an ugly fellow who had a habit of vanishing in a puff of smoke and shooting men in the back. This character was developed about five years ago when Hubbard sat down to see if he could write a story in ten days, a full book of 60,000 words. He made it in eleven days and called the book *Pirate Castle*. In it was a pirate's ghost called the Shark of the Caribbean, the villain of the piece, and it was the shark who haunted the author.

And it was annoying in more ways than one to Hubbard—the novel started to collect rejects in wholesale lots. It went to every magazine that ever printed such stories. It went to every publishing house. It went over the Atlantic and had tiffin with London publishers, and even said skoal with the Scandinavians. But to no avail. Nobody wanted that book, and the ghost kept coming back to bother Hubbard in his sleep.

Well—finally one of the major Hollywood studios bought it and hired the author to write the play, and even then, he wasn't through with it. *Argosy* asked for a rewrite of the novel, a change of editors and another request for a rewrite. Finally the story was buried with honor and lives . . . on the screen.

Back to "Six-Gun Caballero." John Burr is *Western Story*'s editor now and Hubbard admits he has a lot of faith in him. He doesn't get sudden spasms like other editors; all he wants is a good story. It doesn't matter what happens as long as the story will interest the reader. That is sensible editing.

Don Michael, for instance, is not the usual western gunman hero at all but a very smooth lad. That made the story and that is why people will read it. Often, even in a slick paper, an editor will get a formula he likes and then every writer has to adhere to that formula—which drives most any writer into madness.

When I asked L. Ron Hubbard what kind of a fellow is the average writer, he refused to be trapped. Very seldom are they college graduates. Rich man, poor man, beggarman and thief, since O. Henry[1] did time in Ohio, even if there were very extenuating circumstances. That's what makes the game interesting. From one day to another, no editor knows from whence the best story of the year will spring. Editors depend on old-timers, but then writing is a trade as much as plumbing. It has to be learned by practice.

L. Ron Hubbard says a writer's success is his ability to get drunk—on words. And here's good advice, kind listeners, the more a writer writes, the more he can write. Hubbard says if he does 5,000 words today, he can do 10,000 tomorrow. But if he stops for a week it takes another week to get going again. A writer can write himself into a jag of weeks duration. Hubbard recently did a 130,000 words in six days. He mentions Arthur J. Burks as a real speed demon on a typewriter. Burks recently wrote 70,000 words in three days. Quality seems to improve with speed.

"Six-Gun Caballero" was done in 5 days. Five thousand the first day, something like a thousand each of the next three days and twelve thousand the last day.

Well, thanks many times to L. Ron Hubbard. Read his "Six-Gun Caballero" and express your thanks by telling his editor what you think of the yarn. The interest of these top-notchers is greatly appreciated.

Well, writers and readers, our time is really short. Next week we'll be on at 10:00 P.M. and at the same time on succeeding weeks. . . . Come early . . . stay late . . . This is Bob De Haven hoping you'll listen again and tell your friends about this program.

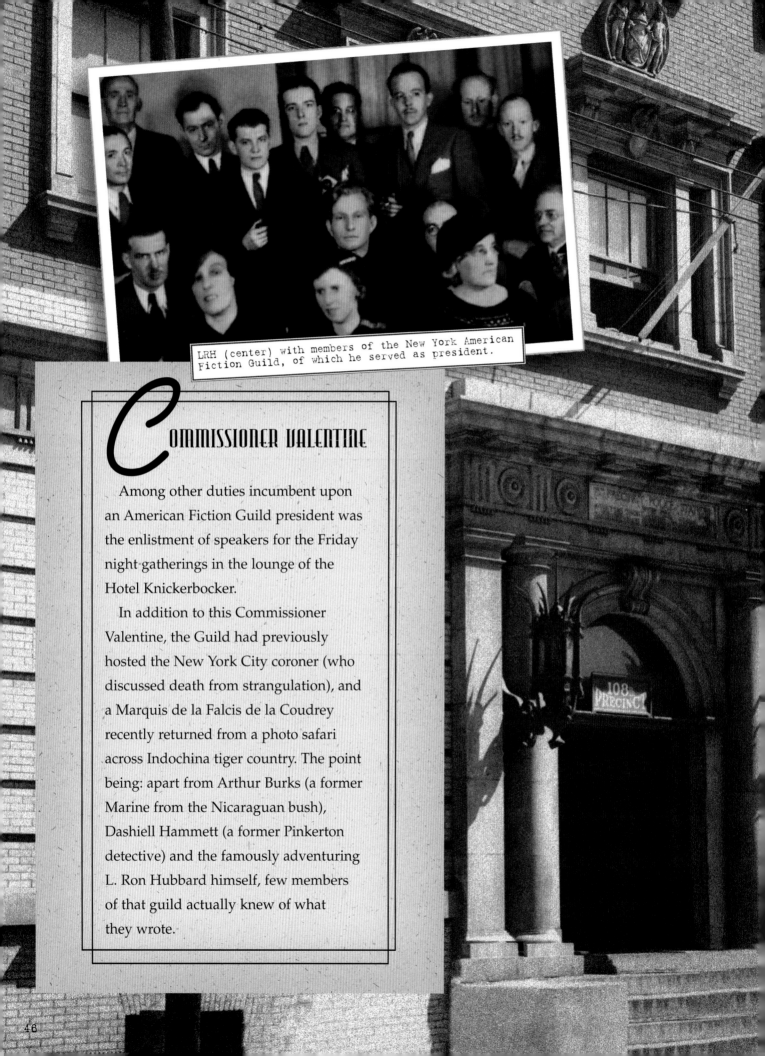

LRH (center) with members of the New York American
Fiction Guild, of which he served as president.

Commissioner Valentine

Among other duties incumbent upon
an American Fiction Guild president was
the enlistment of speakers for the Friday
night gatherings in the lounge of the
Hotel Knickerbocker.

In addition to this Commissioner
Valentine, the Guild had previously
hosted the New York City coroner (who
discussed death from strangulation), and
a Marquis de la Falcis de la Coudrey
recently returned from a photo safari
across Indochina tiger country. The point
being: apart from Arthur Burks (a former
Marine from the Nicaraguan bush),
Dashiell Hammett (a former Pinkerton
detective) and the famously adventuring
L. Ron Hubbard himself, few members
of that guild actually knew of what
they wrote.

AMERICAN FICTION GUILD

40 KING STREET
NEW YORK CITY

November 23, 1935

Commissioner Valentine
Police Department
New York City

Dear Sir:

The New York Chapter of the American Fiction Guild is holding an informal dinner meeting at the Hotel Knickerbocker, December 6, Friday evening at six-thirty.

At the meetings it is customary to have some noted personality of the day address the professional writers of the organization upon some subject touching their work. We have had, for instance, in the past, several noted criminologists whose talks have been of great help to our detective story writers, most of whom try in all sincerity to present the police departments accurately in their stories.

It has been suggested that you might like to deliver your views with regard to the problem of crime. It would not, I assure you, fall on barren ground. Our detective writers reach between fifteen and twenty million impressionable minds a month and it has often been mentioned that fiction might do well to play a hand with the law. Crime stories have always borne the brunt of many attacks, and it is conceivable that they influence crime itself. So far, however, the law itself has done little but condemn detective fiction.

Very few of our detective writers--and by that I mean some of the biggest names in such fiction--have ever seen the inside of a station house. Most of this material is turned out blind. The writers do not seem to realize that they hold a mighty bludgeon of influence with their stories.

While the police departments are critical of newspapers and pay strict attention to newspaper comment, these departments pay little attention to fiction which ranks only second in importance to newspapers.

The fault does not lie wholly with the writers. They do not think that police stations and police agents have time to give out accurate information concerning their work and, as a consequence, the detective writer has molded a model of his own which is quite probably far from the truth.

Recently we considered asking James J. Finn of the Hauptmann[1] case to speak at one of our future meetings, but in discussing detective work we decided that we might make an attempt to better the position of our detective writers.

We know that you are given more than you can possibly do, we appreciate that your time is valuable and that this request might seem a little presumptuous, but there is this to consider: If you, with your position and authority, spoke to us in regard to police work, and extended to our detective writers an invitation to help the law with their work, and if you were to suggest that any station house and precinct was open to their inspection, we are certain that the address would have a greatly desired effect.

You would not, in extending that invitation, deluge your department with any amount of work. There are less than a hundred detective writers of importance in the country. A large share of them will be present at the dinner. But though their numbers are few, this scant hundred write 95 percent of all the detective fiction printed in the country, from the best-selling novel down to the cheapest detective pulp.

It is, therefore, a rather simple task to influence the entire field. Fiction has made the G-man soar to heroic heights in the hands of this group of writers. It was this which suggested to us that we might better our treatment on a closer subject, the police departments of our large cities.

The American Fiction Guild operates primarily for the benefit of today's professional writer, but sometimes we step aside and grasp other urgent work. We fight plagiarism, fraud of all kinds, and so you might say that we're something of a police department ourselves.

Any message you might care to give the New York Chapter of this organization would be relayed promptly to almost every writer of importance in the United States.

We want, frankly, a closer alliance between fiction and fact. We have accomplished that in other fields. The Department of Justice has given writers immeasurable aid so that G-man fiction is gradually becoming accurate and there is, therefore, a better public understanding of that work.

This is, therefore, no idle request that we make. We earnestly desire your presence at this dinner. It is not exactly a social affair and it does not try to achieve social standing. We are men trying to do a sincere job in a sometimes difficult world. Our imaginations give us worldly wealth, and information is highly responsible for whatever prestige we might attain. An address by you and an invitation from you would result, we assure you, in mutual benefit.*

Respectfully,

[signature: L. Ron Hubbard]

L. Ron Hubbard

---

* Although no record of Commissioner Valentine's address appears in the pages of the American Fiction Guild Bulletin, more than one author of detective mysteries was soon turning up with lists of questions for New York Police Department officers.

1. Hauptmann: Bruno Richard Hauptmann, convicted of kidnapping Charles Lindbergh's twenty-month-old son.

*L*ITERATURE FOR BREAKFAST

Quite apart from all else Ron championed in the name of truly *popular* literature, we come upon his modest proposal to the Kellogg Company. Then synonymous with corn flakes, the Kellogg's box had, indeed, stood on every typical American breakfast table while heroic ballads, still penned in Tin Pan Alley, continued to capture the popular imagination. As for his suggestion regarding American presidents and a "classical series, " it just so happens that munching Americans would eventually find something very similar on their cereal boxes.

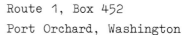

Route 1, Box 452
Port Orchard, Washington

General Manager
THE KELLOGG COMPANY
Battle Creek, Mich.

Dear Sir;

For many a year I have been grossly annoyed by the packaging proclivities of the manufacturers of prepared cereals and, I have reason to believe, I am only one among millions with the same complaint.

However, it has always been a maxim of mine never to criticize unless something better can be suggested. Accordingly, I generated an idea which might or might not be of interest to you.

Every morning, millions of Americans groggily seat themselves at their breakfast table and stare stupidly at the cereal box while stoking themselves with the contents. The cereal box is the fixture of the breakfast table and ranks with ham and eggs in Americanism. But when the consumer begins to imbibe the contents he is also imbibing the intelligence printed upon the box. He reads everything on it. Because it is the brightest thing on the table it commands and gets his attention even though it has nothing to either show or say beyond the lauding of the contents. As the consumer is already oversold on everything under the sun, he cares very little about the advertising.

Some time ago--and perhaps still--you ran a sort of continued story on one of your cereal boxes. But this was a rather wide idea because it is a long time between boxes. Then you had some very short sketches of this and that, but these too were most inadequate.

You labor under the fixation that only children eat cereal and so you plaster the box with subchild objects. It is to be doubted if children form a fifth of the consumers of prepared cereals, and, even if you must still slant toward the child, you can bracket the work to miss the elder eater less widely.

To the point then: you should have something which bears repetitious inspection. Neither continued story, short story nor the lives of great men can answer this test. Once read they are finished and, when the consumer must read them three mornings in a row, they are irksome. Especially are they a source of annoyance to the elder on the third morning because, initially, they were designed wholly for children.

The problem lies mainly in the fact that the box must carry the name and advertising of the cereal with due attention to recipes and what one gets by sending in a box top and ten cents. But this can be circumnavigated handsomely by using a method hitherto unused on any package, so far as I know.

Oil paper used to furnish the outer wrapper of the package. This has now been driven inside, for the most part. But, supposing that you wished to ingratiate your cereal with the most irritable of eaters, how could you avoid placing all the lurid advertising before his fastidious but uncontrollable eyes and still give your package adequate display on the grocer's shelves, if not through the medium of this exterior wrapper? If the inner package contained the cereal's name and the name of its manufacturer in letters only twelve point, they would still be read and received by the consumer at his breakfast--in fact they would be better received.

The box, as it is now presented, could be the same box in appearance on the grocer's shelves with only a slight difference and certainly at no cost greater than its advertising value, if all present matter was printed upon a semitransparent outer cover which could be removed before the box reached the breakfast table. The box itself, in this case, would then carry, in addition to what follows, the name of the cereal and its manufacturer to ensure their being remembered.

Now, for the new box, the face of which would very dimly show through the outside wrapper, there are innumerable things which could be used which would have appeal both to children and elders. The main thing is to make the box so very attractive that it will be a distinct addition to the appearance of the breakfast table so that mama would never forbear to place it boldly thereon--a thing which esthetic mamas do not very often do in the box's present condition.

Once there was an excuse for lurid packaging. Inks and printing methods outlawed any great attempt at handsome presentation. But now, with the improved methods of multicolor printing, when many can be placed at the same time in their exact shades, it becomes possible to cheaply achieve very beautiful results.

First, there could be ballads. There are hundreds and hundreds of them in existence, all of them public property by now. Men always wish, covertly or otherwise, that they knew a string of ballads. However, it is rare to find even an accurate printing of even the most famous of them. "Young Charlotte," "Jesse James," "Casey Jones," "Springfield Mountain," "The Face on the Barroom Floor," and a thousand others are in current knowledge, but few are the people who have read all of them or any of them. On the shelf, the housewife finds the old, familiar package, somewhat changed by the box printing which barely shows through. She buys, as usual, but when she gets home she tears off the printed translucent wrapper and finds something worth looking at. In colorful modern watercolor

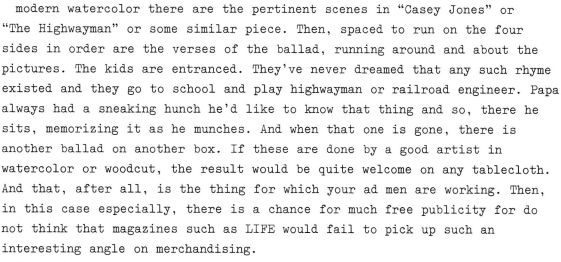

modern watercolor there are the pertinent scenes in "Casey Jones" or "The Highwayman" or some similar piece. Then, spaced to run on the four sides in order are the verses of the ballad, running around and about the pictures. The kids are entranced. They've never dreamed that any such rhyme existed and they go to school and play highwayman or railroad engineer. Papa always had a sneaking hunch he'd like to know that thing and so, there he sits, memorizing it as he munches. And when that one is gone, there is another ballad on another box. If these are done by a good artist in watercolor or woodcut, the result would be quite welcome on any tablecloth. And that, after all, is the thing for which your ad men are working. Then, in this case especially, there is a chance for much free publicity for do not think that magazines such as LIFE would fail to pick up such an interesting angle on merchandising.

Then, for those who might wish to vary the routine, they could see a classical series. You could run a series of famous dramatic paintings on your box with a very, very short description of the picture. The paintings of American history now on display in Washington furnish endless material and, further, mama might like Willie to know his history better and papa really should review it a trifle through such a very pleasant medium. Schoolteachers would be very glad of such a source. And those paintings are not exactly eyesores.

There could follow a dramatization of inventions done rather in illustration style than in the comic strip harshness usually used on such things. The point throughout is to produce on a box a harmonious blend which would place the cereal on the table instead of in bowls before it went to the table. At the bottom, on a colored strip, the cereal's name could be displayed.

There is little use to enumerate the number of things which could be essayed, all achieving the same effect.

Not to be discounted is the psychological effect on the consumer. Digestive and mental functions are closely interlocked. Corn flakes could, in no better way, become synonymous for bravery and gallantry. Anything blatantly approached sooner or later deadens itself by its very commotion. But this is no obvious attempt.

If the function of packaging is to sell more merchandise and to place the merchandise itself upon a higher level, then the double printing of wrapper and box would wipe out its added cost ten times over by the goodwill created. And such a package, I trust, could be protected by process of patent or copyright.

Wishing you success in the New Year, I am,

Sincerely,

L. Ron Hubbard

THE RUSSELL HAYS LETTERS

Among other great friendships born from these years, was the three-decade bond between LRH and fellow author Russell Hays. Hays was a fascinating figure. In addition to the penning of highly authentic westerns, he held several key patents for helicopter rotary systems, coaxed fine skunk cabbage from Kansas dust and occasionally drilled for oil. Needless to say, and notwithstanding a penchant for chewing tobacco and the monosyllabic drawl, he also possessed an exceptionally keen wit. (Ron describes it as "the sticklike quality of a twig-bug, developed to trap the unwary"). Then, too, he harbored a fairly keen interest on questions relating to the human thought process—hence, the later Hays–Hubbard correspondence on Dianetics as provided in *Letters and Journals: The Dianetics Letters*—and had no less to say on the woof and warp of creative writing; hence the letters here.

These letters tells us a lot. Hays has been discussing what he terms the literary "lift," or the plotting of stories according to an emotional curve. LRH responds with an equally elaborate theory on characterization as drawn from actual experience, e.g., "I threw away my dashing lieutenant and substituted a drunken top sergeant. I snatched up a Chinese missionary and wrote him as I knew him." They further have a few choice words on editorial restrictions and a natural aversion to the "main track" of convention—all while proving, as Arthur J. Burks so rightly declared, "No one but a writer can understand a writer's ailments."

Route 1, Box 452
Port Orchard
Washington
December 4, 1937

Dear Russell;

It's been quite a while since I've zipped a letter your way and of course I wouldn't do it unless I had something to tell you about.

And so, with hopes for the health of your family and bank account, I plunge into the subject.

I have just found out something with which to repay that very kind favor of yours anent the "lift" angle on stories, and while I was working this out, I recalled something you said about your work before you slowed down and stopped key pounding. That you did stop has always been a source of puzzlement to me because you are an excellent technician.

This all sounds very serious, but it is serious because I recently found myself heading for the same impasse and after studying the situation out I came to a conclusion which is so ridiculous in its simplicity that it cannot help but be right. And my astonishment is not small that it has not been bannered before this. But I am not bannering it except to you, and as I respected your confidence in the "lift" analysis, respect mine in this....

If you take a squint at an ARGOSY which will be out shortly--I don't know just when and it may be out now-- you'll find ORDERS IS ORDERS, 28,000, China, USMC. In it I adapted movie script writing to fiction writing, which is beside the main point as all my stuff is coming that way today.

But attend! I rolled one, 20,000, called THE CARGO OF COFFINS. It wasn't a very good technical job as I was monkeying with a situation I found in Casanova. It was a very unique piece of styling. But it was actually a second-rater. But ARGOSY ate it without comment.

Attend! ORDERS IS ORDERS is definitely first-rate technically and has plenty of color and suspense.

ARGOSY says nothing about A CARGO OF COFFINS. But when they accepted ORDERS IS ORDERS, they commented to the effect that my Japanese were a shade too villainous, etc., etc., all comment on character as most of my comment has been.

A CARGO OF COFFINS was accepted with this comment, "I think you got a bit more character work on this one than in any of the others you have headed our way recently. . . ."

This is all screwy because the characterization in the latter was definitely lousy. All stock stuff.

Now romps home a western, in which the editor says ". . . also the girl was a very unpleasant person and hardly worth the trouble the hero went to to marry her . . . As you know I like my material a little more conventional than this, especially where the hero and heroine are concerned. That is, I like a heroine our readers can love and admire. . . ."

That western was a pip,[1] take my word for it. Technically it was all to the good. A swell twist to it, smooth writing and, believe it, good <u>characterization</u>.

Now that is the first intelligent comment I have read in four years, although it seemed infuriating at first. That western ed[itor], Lawson, published terrible tripe, published a lot of my stories . . . see "Tinhorn's Daughter" December WESTERN ROMANCES.

I have been gradually going nutty with such stuff. A lousy job would sell, a good job would come back. My best bits of characterization have been slammed home at me. But each time an editor said "characterization" both me and I thought he meant Characterization. And so, distractedly I would improve my <u>methods</u> of characterization and wearily return to the fray. My best plots came home, my best writing. It was enough to send me to the doggy depths and almost did.

I used to get by with pretty second-rate stuff and now I've worked hard to improve my technique, characterization, everything. In the books for which I write I find bad technique, punk characterization. There must be some answer.

So, having explained all this dilemma, and after walking in circles for the last week, I've got an answer which has to be right. My <u>methods</u> of characterization have never been under fire. The poor dumb editors have bitterly assailed them without realizing that they were shooting at the wrong target. They ought to be drowned for a bunch of blundering dopes, but they did succeed in teaching me <u>methods</u> of characterization by yelling about them all the time. I've got the ways and means of characterization too thoroughly catalogued for my own satisfaction that they can't be wrong. That sounds pretty broad, but a man can't help but make progress when he hammers on one subject for years.

These editors were trying to tell me with astonishing blundering that my <u>characters</u> were wrong for their books. Like you, I hated the main track and strove for unusual characters. And the more they yelled, the more unusual my characters became. You went off when you started to glorify your bad men. Remember? You did a fine technical job of that, but the fundamental fact was that a glorified bad man wasn't editorially digestible. And so I arrived at a "law."

1. pip: short for pippin, a highly admired or very admirable person or thing.

Attend! Never write about a character type you cannot find in the magazine for which the story is intended.

Never write about an unusual character.

Experiment with plot, technique, characterization methods, but limit your character exploration to improving those characters which have already appeared.

I am going through my pulps with great thoroughness, cataloguing every character type appearing therein. You will discover that they are very limited. In a western, the villain is thus and so. The heroine is either thus or thus. The hero is emphatically such and so.

This, as I said, is too, too simple to be mentioned. Certainly everybody knows that. But do they?

Is it because writers are generally slow to improve their work? Is it because they usually want the most money for the least work? Is it because they have neither the pride nor ambition necessary to develop to any great extent as a general class? They started in doing something they called "slanting." Certain stories clicked so they kept writing them. They duplicated not only their character types but their plots. The latter was wholly unnecessary, unrequired.

That groundwork cannot be undone.

Lately I applied Newton's three laws to the mass of people, because I'm up here without anybody to talk to and pretty bored generally. The result is useful.

People as a mass obey all the laws of physics. Especially Newton.

Gravitation: They herd into tribes and cities.

Interaction: They tend to oppose any force acting against them as a mass.

Inertia: They tend to remain at rest until that state is overcome by a gigantic force sufficient to start them rolling in a given direction. They tend to keep moving in a straight line as a mass, mentally, and the force of gray matter sufficient to swerve all that composite thought is enormous.

Thus, you have the reason for the fact that every innovator is usually crushed when he tries to oppose the inertia of a people. Witness Paine, Erasmus, Spinoza et al.

Then, who the hell am I to set myself up for a suicidal piece of stream-bucking?

The inertia, moving, of the reading public is a mighty nasty thing to monkey with. Generations of writers have been busily educating this mass to recognize certain character types as being actual types. The mass is led to expect certain things of these characters and will not accept them if those qualifications are not present, or if other bewildering innovations have been added.

As one man I cannot hope to educate the entire mass of people into appreciating smooth technique of character development. I can only give them what they have been having. I can improve that with method and they're none the wiser. They only feel themselves moved or excited.

Do editors know this? Or do they just keep printing the same characters over and over because experience had made them feel-- without making them think--that such and such a character has always gone over great and will therefore continue to do so.

Look over ARGOSY. You'll find the most horrible blunders made by writers in the field of character development. But their characters are a pattern. And despite plot, technique or lack of it, grammar, dialogue . . . in spite of everything, as long as the tempo is right and the story possible and probable, and as long as that character is a pattern character, the yarn will sell. Any number of technical sins are weekly committed by men who should know better and they get by.

All this, says Russell, is pretty obvious stuff. But it took me a long time to figure it out and the conclusion is pretty startling.

No matter what you do in a story, if your characters are pattern characters you can get by beautifully. If you have a gift for fictioneering, attention to character pattern will solve all.

I was going nutty before I thought this up. I recalled with misgivings that a technician like yourself finally stopped. And then I remembered that remark you made about your bad men. And in that and in it alone lies a volume.

I've been hitting the study end of this business pretty hard for a long time and I couldn't conceive the possibility that while I did a polished job on a character he was rejected because of "characterization." Well, I've got the last laugh but you're the only guy I'm telling. I know now that I can have all the fun I want in twisting plots and trying out stunts of technique as long as I use standard characters. Maybe I ought to be kind of bitter about it, maybe I am, but I'm going to put all my energy into making these character types even better by application of method to a recognized hero, heroine, villain or otherwise.

Incidentally, the tip-off to all this for me was that comment about "your Japanese were too 'villainous.'" My Japanese weren't the polite, hissing, bowing, apologetic gents fiction leads us to believe. Unhappily, I knew too many of them in Tsingtao and a military Japanese is a tough customer.

Added tip-off is my utter inability to sell a story which has any connection with my own background. I do it as it is, not as the reading public has been educated to believe that it is. So be it. Reality seems to be a very detested quantity.

Anyway, there it is in solemn array. . . .

Blow the dust off your portable and tell me that everything I've written is pretty obvious so I can write back and tell you ¢%&W¢@&%!

Regards,

Ron

Route I, Box 452
Port Orchard, Washington
December 31, 1937

Dear Russell;

I am deeply insulted on so many counts that you do well to be in
Kansas, me being such an excellent sharpshooter.

To begin, got a beautiful Xmas card from you all, truly thank you
and your lady, which you evidently didn't see sent. . . .

"Orders is Orders" was not quite a jell and you sensed it. I had
a somewhat ordinary plot to begin and suddenly in a flash of revolt
I tossed out my lovely heroine and made her a fan dancer out of
anger for all lovely and impossible heroines. I threw away my dashing
lieutenant and substituted a drunken top sergeant. I snatched up a
Chinese missionary and wrote him as I knew him. I backslapped the
Japanese for stopping me and almost jailing me once in Tsingtao. From
a height of ideal formula, unable to control the impulse, I dragged
the story into muck. And even then I checked that impulse. The result
was, of course, mediocrity.

The best Chinese story I ever wrote was written for my own
amusement. It is the tale of a second officer in Tsingtao harbor,
a crocked engineer and a White Russian prostitute. The scene was a
brothel. I was able to report accurately, had a point to drive, had a
fill of laughing at the phrase "The pathway to sin is hard to desert."

The definition of art--if any definition actually exists--must
certainly contain the phrase, "The artist's conception of. . . ."

You have it neatly when you say that these characters do not exist.
You drive home your point obliquely, as a reversal of your statements
serves as proof for mine.

Go to a boy scout meeting, says you, and test-tube your work. In
itself, that is an excellent idea.

I have noticed a strange thing about my own operations. A kindly
old fellow lent me a Plot Genie once. I was having a bad time building
stories to fit the print. I plotted about three infallibles from that
Genie and tried to write one. I was so sour and dead when I rose from
that mill that I hated myself for days and days.

If anyone begins to analyze foolproof editorial formulas for me,
I also feel nerveless and sagging. Yours happen to be an exception
to this as yours always have been clearly conceived and extremely
interesting for their originality and I take a deep interest in them
for the same reason that you do--mental phenomena.

Your "lift" idea netted me a couple dozens of acceptances.

But, in general, I have only to pick up the A & J,[1] to accidentally read a half-conclusioned writer's mental miscarriage on the subject of commercial writing and something within me turns up its toes and leaves me like London's "vacant shrine."

Having sensed this long ago, I strove to solve what appeared to be an interesting piece of brain reaction.

After weary wading in darkness, I think I have the clear answer.

Even as you, I am a chronic individualist, which trait grows acute and painful whenever the source of my pay is run over into a category of mere mechanical application. I can't work like that. Neither can you.

You and I, to be serious, hold that certain things are true in this world. You have your conception of how people look and act, so have I. We both battle against any conventional tendency. We sullenly regard anything which tends to type anything about us.

The shock of having the last brick pulled from my granary foundation came with these steady criticisms of character. I did not like those characters as they were revolt characters, a will to refuse compliance to an editor, a stubbornness to cling to my own interpretation of life. Hollywood made the tower lean, ARGOSY caused it to topple.

At this writing I have here orders for at least six yarns aggregating about seventy-five thousand words or fifteen hundred dollars. By application of your analysis I could fill those orders swiftly. . . .

Macmillan wants a novel and I have said that I would write it. To begin I am going over to the scene of that novel, Grand Coulee Dam, and loaf for two whole weeks.

And then I am going to begin a story which has been growing bigger and bigger with me day by day. There are no taboos save those against boring. And in the spirit of revolt I can guarantee the quality of that novel. I'll write it long and write it hard and if it is the last time I ever touch finger to key, I am going to pick up Grand Coulee, swing it around and slam it into print with such violence that it can't help but make a big noise. Macmillan's hallmark plus what has accumulated within me for five years, plus a habit of swift writing should make a combination good enough to haul me out of this mire.

I speak bitterly, without any humor, without any relieving lightness. But I am Rip, awake to the fact that I have been in the half-death of sleep for five years.

Know that I have enjoyed myself only twice in that span because I was able to embattle my wits without fear of sullen silence or lack of understanding. Encinitas, for a while, and then New York for a very short time. . . .

Last week I remembered flinging myself out of my bunk at the age of eighteen, dressing while it was demanded of me why I refused to return to school. And I answered, aghast, "There isn't any time! I've got so much to do, so little time to do it. . . ."

Yes. And that same spirit has vanished. But not so far into the yesterdays that I can fail to recover its meaning and the sensation of

1. A & J: AUTHOR AND JOURNALIST, a writer trade magazine.

having it. Not so far that I fail to understand the method of getting it.

Certainly not sitting here on a hilltop pounding out my brains at two cents a word. I have learned enough of my trade, have developed a certain technique. But curbed by editorial fear of reality and hindered by my own revolt I have never dared loose the pent flame, so far only releasing the smoke.

I <u>know</u> what I can put into my book. Plot and lead characters at hand, research remaining on the spot where the writing will be done. Strangely enough, now that I am working only to please myself I automatically evolve some of the factors which I have refused to accept upon command. My hero is going to scrap his way straight up the ladder in spite of hell and the course of his going will make dramatic--not melodramatic--telling.

I am sick of pulling my one-two, my verbal right, my energy left. And when I finish that story, the paper is going to be charred by the blast of its composition.

The novel field is so clear one pities the stumbling novelists for not availing themselves of the latitude which they are allowed. Certainly "Romeo Reverse" by Scurvy Gallon was bought only because no better yarns were being written. And, at the risk of great conceit unless you have read that gentleman, Wilder,[2] Madam Mitchell[3] et al., if a writer trained in the impact of syllables and on the rampage could not blow them all down with one hot breath, I err and know nothing of my art.

And here again we have analysis, but of a kindlier kind. Verbose, pseudo-intellectualism has been badly handled by all the above. Macmillan is panting for a bestseller. The task is simple, the field gaping. I am mad enough to write it. . . .

It does a man good to get really disgusted. Convention brands it variously: bitter and sour grapes. But five years ago I was a sky-rocket for enthusiasm and now I discover that somebody has been holding my hand to keep me from lighting the fuse. I'm convinced that I must return to that go-to-hell, "Anywhere but Here" existence. I started traveling when I was three weeks old. I lone-wolfed it through my teens. I managed to poke into live volcanoes and icebergs and Ladrone[4] burying grounds and Peking hock shops. . . .

Pulling punches is not healthy. Biding by the chain when the chain scrapes sores is the mark of the fool, the ignoble man, the groveler in the dust before the idols of the mass. And I've been pulling punches and biding chains. For fear men would laugh I have not said what I have thought. For fear men would be offended, I have stifled opinions which sizzled in my throat. And I know I have cared too much for that which is worth too little. . . .

It's late and tonight I am supposed to go to a party so I had better knock off some sleep. I sure wish there was a chance of blasting you out of the land where the sun never shines and back into the never-never country.

Best regards,

Ron

2. Wilder: Thornton Wilder (1897-1975), American novelist and playwright.
3. Madam Mitchell: Margaret Mitchell (1900-1949), American author who wrote GONE WITH THE WIND.
4. Ladrone: also known as the Mariana Islands, in the Pacific, which includes Guam.

Russell Hays

Misterfer Ron Hubbard
NYC, NY
USA

Hullo there:

I am very sorry to state that I have nothing to ride, razz, or pensively contemplate about yourself, immediate fambly, labors, or fate. Whatever the setup in the city, it all sounds very mysterious. Now Ronny, my boy, are you sure you are associating with er—respectable peoples? You ain't havin' no truck with gangsters, be you?

Wal, pardner, I read that there story in this here WESTERN STORY magazine; and dang it it weren't all right. No sour notes. Seriously, I envy you your ability to bat out that smooth a yarn. Of the writers who bust into the pulps or slicks either, there is just about one in ten who ever reach the level of consistently flowing out smooth ones avoiding sour something or others. In a way, the knack is like Bing Crosby's singing. His is only another voice, and by operatic standards a rather lousy voice, but smooth and no jar to it. A pleasant comfortable sound, no straining, no screeching, and no interpreter to tell you what he is singing about. Mebbe I'm just lowbrow and don't know what singing is, but I notice a heap of cash customers agree with me.

Things down on the farm are much as usual, a thousand things more to do than one shiftless being like myself can hope to challenge. Never before in my life have I been so trapped. Economically and climatically, I realize that it is very silly for me to continue staying here. I think I can guess at the reason I continue doing so. As a child, batting about the country with my mother, this place here where three generations of my forebearers had lived and died, came to be a symbol of sorts to me. That peculiar thing which as a child I never had, a home.

It is the damned, most intangible thing I have ever bucked up agin. I am the only one of my generation left here. Even the fellows I played with here as a child have all drifted away. I have only lived here a small fraction of my life, I have not a single close friend here, and yet everybody in this end of the county knows me by my first name. What I may have been or wish to be, means absolutely nothing to them. I am a symbol of something or other very close to the soil. I am the Hays who lives in the big house out at Blackjack. I am the boss-man by that illogical, unjustified thing called inheritance. I have a nasty feeling that if I pull out from here I am letting somebody down. . . .

Doggone, I am getting sleepy. Just can't take this night life. Incidentally, my red-haired friend when you return to home and fireside it isn't going to cost you any more to get routed through Kansas City, hence you can drop off and tell me any new and vulgar stories you may be collecting at this time.

I yam, sinceripatedly,

Russell

Route One, Box 452
Port Orchard, Wash.
October 20, 1938

Dear Russell;

Just why I am inditing this epistle to you I am not sure because I hadn't ought on account of copious copy which lies in wait behind the eyes to pounce forth into immortal print--or is that "immoral"?

I have been cursing myself for a bum--which is nothing new--due to my seeming inability to get anything written which will magnetize the lucre. In truth I am having far too pleasant a time rolling around here swamping out woods and fumbling the idea of amusing myself by building a log cabin. This is the lotus land and if one doesn't watch, he hears the clock strike eighty before he thinks he has left twenty.

I made a flying trip to Seattle yesterday to get some things and stuff and incidentally to have the yearly overhaul on the mill. This time I added a nice little stroke counter as a sort of protest against Street & Smith's late habit of being particular with their word counts--they annoy me. Now I can say "Cyclometer counted--9,919,334 words." Little countometer on the back of the machine rolls up one count for every ten strokes including space strikes. A word averages five with space, so I am told. I'll have to check that.

Haven't seen Mein Herr Egdvedt[1] since my return but have been planning to drop in on him. Yore old friend Eddie Allan is testing this new flying fortress. See his Satevepost[2] article? Never seen one of these test pilots yet that didn't have to chuck his weight around in print. . . .

By the way, it worried me for some time that I had no particularly original method of presentation for the book and last week I thunk one up. I kind of sighed when I did because I knew I would have to do it that way and it meant an awful lot of revamping on the stuff already done. However I have run out of excuses and so I think I may have to get to work on it most anytime. I was further annoyed by another bid on that Coulee Dam book, Lords of the Roaring River, and if I do that I suppose I'll really go whole dog and write a piece of Americana two hundred thousand words long at least. . . .

Best regards,

1. Mein Herr Egdvedt: Mr. Egdvedt, C. L., president of Boeing Aircraft Company, 1933-1939.
2. Satevepost: popular American national magazine, Saturday Evening Post.

*L*etters from a Literary Season in Manhattan

By early 1939, and firmly at the center of the pulp fiction realm, Ron had established a semipermanent residence in New York City. In consequence, and quite in addition to the usual exchange with editors, we now come upon his letters to friends and family still residing in Washington and Montana.

Nothing so bespeaks the literary life as these letters from Manhattan: the elation mixed with drudgery, the inspiration broken by a dry spell, the occasional nod to the masters and the "write a yarn, disburse funds, think up a yarn, write a yarn . . . Lord!" Lest the titles of works referenced here are not immediately familiar, those "yarns" still stand as among the most memorable in the whole of popular fiction. For having signed on with Street & Smith to infuse a mechanistic science fiction with a new and vibrant human element, these were the days of "Final Blackout," "The Tramp" and "The Dangerous Dimension." While in the pages of Street & Smith's *Unknown*, we find such pillars of modern fantasy as "Fear," "The Ghoul" and "Death's Deputy."

Additionally of interest here: We have elsewhere discussed how the bulk of LRH literary profits went to the exploration and research culminating in the 1950 release of *Dianetics: The Modern Science of Mental Health*. Point of fact: above the desk on which he pounded out his letters from this period hung a nautical chart of a British Columbian passage to Alaska where, in the autumn of 1940 and wholly funded from the stories referenced here, he conducted his famed ethnological research among north coast Indian tribes.

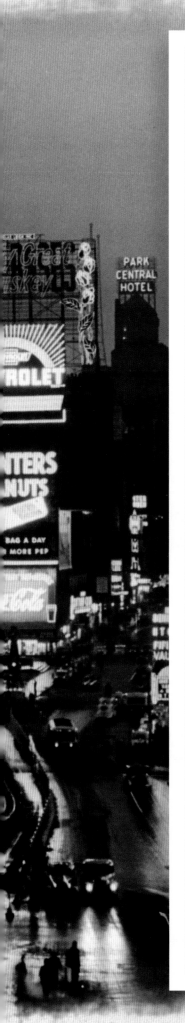

HOTEL KNICKERBOCKER.

Knickerbocker Hotel
New York City
Sunday
July 24, 1938

. . . Strangely enough, having grown extremely sour on the subject of writing--which must be worn off one way or another--I took a brush in hand. I am somewhat astounded to see what can be done with watercolor. Of all the mediums, Matt[1] said it was the one I should not tackle first so, of course, I tackled it. My draftsmanship isn't bad at all and my composition seems to be pretty good. It bears out my contention that medium doesn't matter when a guy is bound and determined to walk into the creative fields. The pity of it in this case is that I waited so darned long before I began to study such things. Of course this painting is a momentary release but just the same it is most exciting. I finally figured out what was this thing called the creative instinct. God probably creates energy. Man converts energy only. With energy God creates all manner of things. And because every form of life is somehow a duplication of the Self, then man begins to approach God's function when he sets out and creates wholly from the stuff of which dreams are made. In other words the approach to godliness does not lie behind the altar but in the province of creation itself. Hence man's excitement at creating anything from ditches to art...

Thus, we can follow out along that line of reasoning and arrive at some very interesting conclusions which indicate a great many apparently disharmonious elements in living.

I smear some paint on a sheet of paper. I put a soaring plane on the lip of a scud cloud and crack the lightning inside the cloud and light up the earth with greenish-yellow tones and label the picture "Excitement." Or I take a man and a horse and a woman and weave them together to construct activities in a world which is existing nowhere but in my own brain. Capturing my own dreams in words, paint or music and then seeing them live is the highest kind of excitement just so long as any of these things are wholly mine, untrammeled by other opinions and unchanged by other hands. A writer is furious "beyond all reason" to have an editor change a single word of his text. But now I think I know the reason. The editor has denied the writer the right to wholehearted creation and ownership of a world of his own construction. A piece of art then ceases to become a piece of art the instant it ceases to be the product of one mind. Naturally nobody is nearly as interested in one of my stories as I am myself. Nobody will see anywhere near as much in a smear of my paint as I will myself. Therefore the critic is not only unwanted but is actually functioning something on the order of a grave robber...

I recall my jealous guardianship of my California vegetable garden. It actually pained me to have anyone touch it or to have to accept advice on it. I didn't really want admiration. The thing in itself was wholly sufficient . . . and so it is with my pages. We must always better them the next time, always strive for perfection in them because if we achieve perfection then we have come as close to the activity of the self as a mortal can get. . . .

Ron

Ron

1. Matt: Hubert "Matty" Mathieu, Greenwich Village artist, painter and close friend of LRH.

Hotel Knickerbocker

Hotel Knickerbocker
New York City
September 14, 1939

. . . I am composing one for Johnny.[1] He and I went into a huddle yesterday and out of it came a theme for a title, DEATH'S DEPUTY. He and I threshed around until we got the idea of a man who officiates, all unwillingly, for the god of destruction. Without volition on his part he causes accidents. No blame can actually be traced to him but he is always, in some small way, responsible. Incidentally, the elimination of such "accident-prones" from large firms has appreciably diminished the accident toll. There are people, then, who seem to be magnets for destruction. Although rarely touched themselves, things happen all around them. One man in a trucking firm was on the scene of seven fatal accidents. As soon as he was removed from the firm the accidents ceased! And yet he had never been a direct or even indirect cause of those accidents so far as physical fact went. His helper, for instance, was in a truck body while this accident-prone stood on the walk. A man fell from the twenty-eighth floor and killed the helper. At another time a motorist ran thirty feet off a road just to strike this accident-prone's truck and kill himself--with no damage to the accident-prone. Seven incidents like that, one after another and the jinx still follows. According to this, then, there is some basis for the maritime Jonah[2]--and in the Navy there is a man who has survived every major sinking in the past twenty years! And was twice the sole survivor. . . . There are, then, men to whom accidents occur, affecting those in their vicinity. And such is the story DEATH'S DEPUTY. . . .

Ron

1. Johnny: John W. Campbell, Jr.
2. In maritime circles, the statement "maritime Jonah" is
   used to describe a man who brings ill fortune to a ship.

Hotel Knickerbocker

Knickerbocker Hotel
New York City
October 12, 1939

. . . Yesterday I heard that John had bought my last and so I am starting today on BLACKOUT, a story of Europe after the war is done.

And so, beginning, I found that the typewriter wasn't working any too well. A mechanic had cleaned it a week or two ago and it hadn't worked right after that. So I made adjustments in tensions and now I feel like I am all thumbs on it. In fact I have never had it run quite so badly--which is encouraging when one is about to begin on a long one. However I suppose it will mainly be a matter of learning the new touch, and the old one was very, very bad.

I think I should probably do better to write this one in pencil and then copy it as I go along. That is a terrible lot of work but, somehow, I seem to get more kick out of writing that way. It does not take me very long to turn them out on the typewriter but neither, anymore, are they so very good. . . .

Here it is almost supper time and I have not yet started my story. I must have worked on this mill for something like four hours and as yet I haven't gotten the touch right. But poor old Inky just had to be cleaned. I wish, when they go about fixing this mill, the mechanics would leave the tensions alone. But they never do.

I have supper with Matt during the first four evenings of the week. Then he takes off for Pennsylvania and appears again on Monday, having left Friday afternoon. In about ten days I am going down with him for a weekend, but I have to get out two stories first, each twenty thousand words. This BLACKOUT and then one for Florence.[1]

The same old story, over and over. Write a yarn, disburse funds, think up a yarn, write a yarn . . . Lord! . . .

I think I'll get my shoes on (still a hillbilly) and go down to dinner. Matt ought to be around about now. . . .

Ron

Ron

1. Florence: Florence McChesney, editor of Five Novels Monthly.

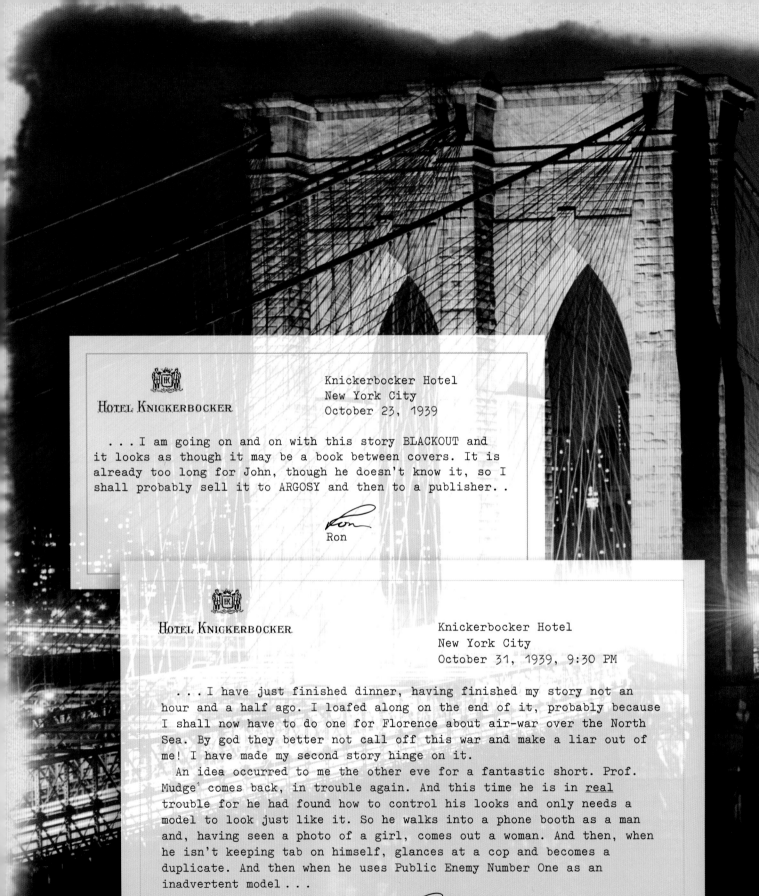

HOTEL KNICKERBOCKER

Knickerbocker Hotel
New York City
October 23, 1939

. . . I am going on and on with this story BLACKOUT and
it looks as though it may be a book between covers. It is
already too long for John, though he doesn't know it, so I
shall probably sell it to ARGOSY and then to a publisher. .

Ron

HOTEL KNICKERBOCKER

Knickerbocker Hotel
New York City
October 31, 1939, 9:30 PM

. . . I have just finished dinner, having finished my story not an
hour and a half ago. I loafed along on the end of it, probably because
I shall now have to do one for Florence about air-war over the North
Sea. By god they better not call off this war and make a liar out of
me! I have made my second story hinge on it.

An idea occurred to me the other eve for a fantastic short. Prof.
Mudge[1] comes back, in trouble again. And this time he is in <u>real</u>
trouble for he had found how to control his looks and only needs a
model to look just like it. So he walks into a phone booth as a man
and, having seen a photo of a girl, comes out a woman. And then, when
he isn't keeping tab on himself, glances at a cop and becomes a
duplicate. And then when he uses Public Enemy Number One as an
inadvertent model . . .

Ron

1. Prof. Mudge: the main character in LRH's "The Dangerous Dimension."

. . . I am all set to put the nose to emery once again. Johnny is short on shorts for both books so, as I am already Rene LaFayette on "The Indigestible Triton," I shall also be, no doubt, Michael DeWolf and perhaps Kurt von Rachen. Maybe I should shift that to Mikkel DeWolf or Mickale and thus run my pseudonyms on the foreign pattern. . . .

So you are reading the classics, are you? Good going. I know you combed them all once but that was in the yesterday when you hadn't begun to think of stories as jigsaw puzzles but as entertainment. Magazine stories, especially the love stories in slick, are about as difficult in construction and presentation as . . . Tinkertoy men--built in two seconds without any change whatever except in the writer's mood. Love in the slick--or most any other thing in slick--is dependent wholly upon draping the simple frame gracefully. There is a type of feeling which is good but once seen it is always simple. Character delineation is too naive for a second glance in slick. Strangely I don't think I could do the stuff for it requires a certain mood which I don't seem to possess. A sort of lazy carelessness which irks me. And so when I see people getting a kick out of magazines I find it very uncomplimentary to their brain power for they become a "reader." Slick is cute and darling at times but never anything but superficial entertainment, mediocre on all sides. I believe tougher jobs have begun to crop up in fantasy than slick ever printed. And if you want something in plot structure, read SLAVES OF SLEEP. I don't dare monkey much with character because it always gets me into hot water. But I think TARANPANG or McGlincy[1] stand up rather well. You might, by the way, send me TARANPANG with a couple extra sheets of the paper it was written upon. Maybe I can sell it now. But anyway, for character, Dickens' satire can't be topped. For tone and mood and objective attained, they don't come better than Poe. And for sheer structure out of incident alone Daudet[2] and Zola[3] are peers. For style Washington Irving is on the peak, for wit Shakespeare, for nonsense Carroll, for psychology Dostoevski. My ambitions do not go into any of these but I like to see what they could do with a given problem. Reading them for entertainment is nonsense unless one is entertained intellectually. Any gift of gab I have seems to be the ability to make a whole story run in moving scenes, dovetailing character and action and working all things out in action terms. That is the goal of the action writer. . . .

Of all the ghastly goulash ever gabbed, radio has the most choice. The Lone Ranger et al. are too idiotic to be given air space but America is doing its level worst to reduce any culture it might evolve by so bombarding the brains of the population with bunk that, before long, everyone will be numb to anything and everything. Senses can be so overloaded with messages that the brain no longer bothers to sort any of them and the process of thought becomes muddled by consequence. The overdose of blah on the radio will result, before long, in the standardization of ideas to the end of killing all ideas. . . .

Ingenuity is at a low and sorry ebb. There is something strangely soothing and satisfying about fairy tales and far lands but there is nothing but brutal degeneration in a radio serial. It does not stimulate the imagination but envelops the interest to the exclusion of imagination. It is canned thought. And veddy, veddy lousy thought it is. Those things aren't even well plotted and they have a tendency to throw logic out of gear. . . .

Leave radio to the mechanics that don't have to think and have nothing with which to think anyway. Its news and a little of its music are quite sufficient to justify its existence. . . .

1. McGlincy: a character in LRH's BUCKSKIN BRIGADES.
2. Daudet: Alphonse Daudet (1840-1897), French novelist.
3. Zola: Emile Zola (1840-1902), French novelist.

LRH

Knickerbocker Hotel
New York City
January 18, 1940

    I have been so upset about a story for the past few days that I have not written . . . not wanting to even touch this mill. However I finally got the plot of it licked and am doing research upon it. . . .

    The story will be named PHANTASMAGORIA[1] and the theme is, "What happened to Dwight Brown on the day he cannot remember?" Twenty-four hours lost from a man's life. And if I handle it properly it will be something Dostoevski might have done. He strives to locate his deeds while missing everywhere but in the right place, for he fears to look there. He is surrounded, day by day, by more terror and apparitions as his solutions are gathered about him only to become hollow and half seen. He knows, deep down, that the day he recognizes his deeds of the day he cannot remember, on that day he shall die. And, having gone mad he has to choose between being mad forever and being dead. And if you don't think that one was a tough one at which to arrive and now plot by incident . . . ! And John Campbell all the while drumming new suggestions at me and insisting I use them . . . ! And five conflicting stories to be woven into one . . . !!!!!!

Ron

Ron

1. PHANTASMAGORIA: published as FEAR in <u>Unknown</u> magazine, July 1940.

Knickerbocker Hotel
New York City
January 28, 1940

    I tried, today, to start PHANTASMAGORIA, having fully outlined it last night. But for some reason I could not think connectedly enough or establish a sufficient mood. It is a pretty dolorous story and so I suppose I had better tell it very calmly and factually, without striving to dwell on mood. . . .

    I've been . . . trying to coax up a certain tone for the story. And I think a nice, delicate style is best suited. Paint everything in sweetness and light and then begin to dampen it, not with the style, but with the events themselves. In other words lead the reader in all unsuspecting and then dump the works on his head. Show very little true sympathy and do not at all try to make the facts worse than they are but rather make light of them. Oh hell! This is such a hard story! But I can see a sleepy college town with spring and elms and yawning students and a man just back from an ethnological expedition, called to take over from a professor who has become ill. A man suited to quiet solitude with a certain still idealism about him, who has come back to his home and his wife and is trying anxiously to fit into the picture which he so long ago left. If told almost dispassionately the thing ought to be good. In other words, I'll just write it. For I can't work up a gruesome mood. Ah, for a few days out of my adolescence! The character must take it all mildly, that's the easiest way. How I hate to make anyone "emote"! . . .

Ron

Ron

243 Riverside Drive
New York City
Friday the 23rd of February 1940

. . . This place up here is a bit of "all right." Sunlight and fresh air
and the river and a chop suey joint that serves good chop suey up on Broadway
and a bar restaurant on Columbus Avenue that serves three lamb chops for fifty
cents with the trimmings. I won't be here into the time for hot weather for that
is probably the only drawback this place has. But that isn't worrying me with
snow all over the place.

I have a little cubicle fixed up in the corner as always. I got some monk's
cloth—paid a total of three bucks for it—and a post of 2 x 2 and some curtain
rods. By facing my desk out from the corner, I could then attach the five-foot
post to the back right-hand corner of my desk, the curtain rods to the post and
so back to the wall and the place is quite nice for it dulls out all sound, even
of the mill. Underfoot I have a Belgian rug about half an inch thick and just
big enough to fill up this space. It gives the table here a little too much
bounce but I can get used to that quickly enough.

Down at Street & Smith's day before yesterday I had quite a time for WILD WEST
WEEKLY wants some stuff from me and, accordingly, I am today starting upon a
short for them just to feel out the reaction. THE SHADOWS is the working title.
Then Jack Burr and I are tearing through the old dime novel library in search of
data on the early life on the Missouri and I'm going to do a 20,000 worder on
the subject for him. He gave me the first of the original Jesse James series as
printed by Street & Smith and there's quite a kick to the stuff at that. S&S . . .
has about six miles of shelves filled with the old dime novels and printed almost
every one of any importance. They are nearly all collectors' items now and I
could only get them by working with Jack. He had a terrible time trying to trace
down the man who has the say about them and then all he could get was a promise
of a catalogue. So today I suppose I should really go downtown and take a squint
at that catalogue. However, I have one to do for Florence before I can start, and
this short.

Ron

243 Riverside Drive
New York City
March 2, 1940

. . . I am doing one now for Florence but it goes very slowly. I did a
fantasy Western this week, a novelette, but the pay won't be so good if it
comes through at all. John wants "grim" stories these days like FEAR. He
always wants again what I have just given him. I wish I had time to do
REDHEAD FROM KAINTUCKY for Cosmo.[1] Maybe I will have time. I don't know.
Hell of it is, I know that the check for it would be all the money I would
need for this entire period of work but still I am scared of using up time
on it.

Made inquiry about Inky's turn-in the other day and discovered she was
worth $30. She was running something awful but as soon as a salesman came
up and began to run her down she picked right up and is now going great
guns. Temperamental typewriter of a temperamental master. . . .

Ron

1. Cosmo: short for Cosmopolitan magazine.

New York City
March 10, 1940

. . . My story is going very slowly. I was supposed to have had the thing finished by tonight but somehow I just couldn't do much writing over this weekend. Maybe the state of my hands had something to do with it. When I awoke Saturday morning they were a mass of bruises though they are almost wholly well now. You see, it's this way. Fletcher had a half housewarming, cocktails at five. And I left the place at one AM along with most of the guests. The thing was definitely a success for nobody got really drunk and everybody had a very fine time. The hands come in because of Fletcher's purchases in Havana.[1] He brought back most of the instruments necessary to the construction of a rhumba band, complete with voodoo drums. Well, I must say that I never knew I could really drum before though I had tried drums a few times in the Indies. Hand playing a drum is quite different from stick-beating it. The amount of rhythm one can extract from a drum with the hands is remarkable. A fellow named Bill had a piano accordion and so he and I and a shifting group of others made the welkin ring. We had everyone doing rhumbas including the bartender. And John Clark says that when he came at six, there I was playing the two-hand drums (they are connected, you see) and when he left at midnight the last thing he saw was me playing the drums. Everyone wanted to know where I learned how to play voodoo drums so I was smart and kept my mouth shut. I am very definitely going to have a couple such drums sent up from Havana. All by themselves they can do very strange things to an audience. They can throb and moan and wail and roll and thunder and whisper like a parade of ghosts. But I paid with a pair of swollen hands. I did not drink much but I got awfully drunk on drum music.

Seems I can't hit the keys right even yet. I seem to have done things to my hands beyond bruising them.

I have a nice story to write soon as I finish this one. About a corpse that would like to be friendly. And then I have a couple more shorts to do in a hurry. And then maybe, if I can think of one, a novel, plus a 20,000 worder for Burr.[2] . . .

Played poker last night at Sprague's.[3] The "Interstate Iniquity Association." I lost seventy-five cents so I guess I am still very lucky . . .

1. In addition to author Fletcher Pratt's "Havana Night," extra-literary affairs included the flying of experimental kites with Saturday Evening Post illustrator Hubert "Matty" Mathieu, BB gun tournaments with the likes of Norvell "The Spider" Page, and ice-skating evenings at Rockefeller Center with any number of others from the hard-driven ranks of the pulp-fiction team.
2. Burr: Jack Burr, editor of Western Story magazine.
3. Sprague: L. Sprague de Camp, writer.

Ron

243 Riverside Drive
New York City
March 19, 1940

. . . This afternoon David Vern, who has been sent to NY by Ziff-Davis in Chicago, called to ask for a short story in a hurry. I was supposed to be starting one for Florence again but I sidetracked it for a day and so am getting out THE CASTAWAY for South Sea Stories. He said he could not guarantee acceptance and it is only for a penny but fifty bucks is fifty bucks and I need the change of writing something like it. It's a pretty good yarn . . .

Ron

243 Riverside Drive
Gnu Yawk
March 21, 1940 2:40 PM

. . . I should be starting another for Florence but instead . . . finished THE CASTAWAY in the small hours. . . .

THE IRON DUKE should be five thousand deep when I quit tonight, for it is due Monday and I want the check Saturday. Besides I have a stack of stuff to do for Johnny. Then S&S broke down and opened its files to me (almost the first time in history that they did that for anybody) and so I am being handed the Buffalo Bill series ten or twelve books at a time. It is much better stuff than the public generally supposes for Prentiss Ingraham actually was a scout with Buffalo Bill and ranged the whole West for the entire early part of his life. So there is material to burn there. . . .

Ron

243 Riverside Drive
New York City
March 25, 1940

. . . Everybody in New York seemed to be blue yesterday. Every phone call I got was deep indigo-Jack Burr, Willy Ley, John Campbell. And so I guess it was just a sweep of the town from leaden skies and drizzling, chilly rain.

I am now going to try to do a short called THE ALKAHEST. It is a very short story and may or may not go over but I want to warm up for a couple novelettes, one for Florence, one for WILD WEST WEEKLY, one for John and then maybe a novel for John. I am finding that I can't drill along as steadily as I thought I could and so now I have to put in several consecutive days' work come what may in order to cancel out the last few days of staring into the fog. . . .

By the end of the week I hope to have put twenty-five thousand over the mill. . . .

Ron

243 Riverside Drive
New York City
March 25, 1940

. . . Yesterday I had a little hard luck with Inky. The tape which carries back the carriage return broke right in the middle of THE IRON DUKE. No, it was Saturday afternoon, right after the IBM office closed. Anyway I sewed it up with needle and thread and it worked for a long time until I finally tried to adjust it. Then it broke in another place. I must have spent five or six hours over the weekend fixing that tape. Today, about one, a mechanic came up and put on a new tape and a few other things and now, of course, I have the dubious pleasure of trying to accustom myself to the new feel of the keyboard, with seven thousand words to do before I am finished tonight. However Inky got herself some new type in spots and the rest aligned and so the type probably looks much better EVEN IF SHE DOESN'T FEEL BETTER TO MY FINGERS. Damn it, it jumped to caps when I was fooling with it. And to top that, last night when I was making me something to eat I cut my finger, the right index, on a piece of paper so that I am very much aware of it. But the story has to be in . . . and so I am skating along and to hell with it. . . .

Tomorrow-or rather, this afternoon I am going down to research data for the KIDNAPPED CHARACTER or whatever the title may prove to be. I have to check history and so on at the Public Library. . . .

Ron

Ron

243 Riverside Drive
New York City
March 28, 1940

. . . Got the okay today on THE IRON DUKE. Florence was ill but dragged herself down to the office just to put it through, for she needed something for a cover. However the front office would not allow her to use "anything foreign" so I don't get a cover again.

Tonight I am going to start to roll the KILKENNY CATS, second of a series of shorts. Then perhaps tomorrow I shall start upon THE ALKAHEST another short for the same market, though the first is under the old name of Kurt von Rachen.

Otherwise I am a bit bored. I have been reading Buffalo Bill and the stuff is pretty crude, so much so that it gives me a stale flavor. Ingraham is overrated in his knowledge of the West I know now for he never gives out any information and no description of the country. A rifle is "of the pattern used at that time." Etc. He avoids any specific data and is therefore rather useless in source.

This mill isn't running any too well again but I guess it will get heated up after a while. Feels sort of draggy to my fingers and persists in not striking or striking too much. . . .

Ron

Ron

243 Riverside Drive
New York City
April 6, 1940

. . . I am waiting for the maid to get out of here as well as Lavatory Sam, guardian of the can who always creeps in with her and surreptitiously swamps the bath. His real name is George but I can never see him without remembering a song about Lavatory Sam . . .

The radio is going with some sweet music. I am allergic to swing, particularly since I eat in bars with coin phonographs howling. The food is good and cheap but my nerves pay heavily. I cook breakfast and lunch and generally eat out. In a week or so I shall probably begin eating down at the Knickerbocker for dinner because Matty has been kicking and I'd just as soon. As a matter of fact I am lonesome and need a break in my day.

Just finished breakfast and it is three-thirty PM. I couldn't start that story and as it is due Monday I now have mill-fright at the amount of working I shall have to do in the next few days. The maid drops things. I just heard something crash.

Well, I paused while the maid finished up. And then I phoned Post and Campbell. The former and I went around and around about a rate. I want to do one in that direction. It's a plot which might run twenty thousand and John can't take it at more than eight thousand. John, further, has his heart set on something "grim" and I don't like to write them at that for they are very tiring and I don't think they are very good. Post says my rate is listed at 1 1/4 cents but sho[1] I never got that from ARGOSY. He thinks it is wrong too. Anyway he says he'll pay 1 1/2 cents if he likes the yarn. I want this market again for an outlet about Alaskan fishing stories.

I had better get going now on SABOTAGE IN THE SKY or whatever I'll call it. For time flyeth....

Ron

P.S.: A static search party just located my mill and it is raising hell with the radios of refugees who are trying to find out how the war is going. I have changed a connection in the mill which is supposed to keep it from kicking back into the line but it is possible that I may have to go back to the Knickerbocker for I can't stay where I can't write and they tell me they'll turn off my juice! However I have the situation under control for today at least.

1. sho: an exclamation expressing contempt, impatience or disapproval.

ᴛ WILIGHT OF THE PULPS

With the advent of the Second World War, and Ron's commission in the United States Navy as skipper of antisubmarine corvettes, his literary life sadly ground to a halt. "I am even unwilling to write these days," he confessed in the winter of 1944. Then wistfully added, "but more and more I am beginning to be determined about writing." What immediately followed from that determination were two historical romances, "written in bits" as a "practice run," and presently unpublished. By late December 1945, however, we find him rather more determinedly informing New York agent Lurton Blassingame, "I have begun a writing business once more."

It was a fairly heroic effort. For notwithstanding his claim to "normalcy," he still suffered grievously from wounds sustained in action. To wit: the muzzle flash of a deck gun had left him legally blind, while shrapnel fragments in hip and back had left him all but lame. In consequence, he could barely seat himself at a typewriter, could not focus on a printed page and, for that matter, could not discern the pages of his own books.

His immediate solution was the Soundscriber Dictaphone and hired stenographer remarked upon in letters to the ever-loyal Leo Margulies of *Standard Magazines*. With the restoration of his health—pursuant, incidentally, to his application of early Dianetics techniques—he continued to employ both Dictaphone and typist in the interest of high-speed production. (Although even at his physical worst, he had still managed some thirty thousand words a month; while by 1947, he healthily resumed his prewar rate—an astonishing seventy thousand words at barely three days a week).

As further evidenced in letters here, however, these were plainly transitional days, with *Unknown* by the boards, *Astounding* in hiatus and the pulps soon drowning in a wash of paperbacks—hence, the LRH requests for a Street & Smith release of rights for republication in hardback. Then, too, and even if letters to the likes of Campbell scarcely allude to the fact, Ron was soon to entirely devote himself to final steps of research towards Dianetics. Hence, the references to his Commodore Deluxe trailer, "tricked up as a writing office," and otherwise the perfect vehicle with which to crisscross the country in search of test cases. Hence, too, the reference to his "writing schedule" as separate to an unmentioned research schedule.

Pasadena, California
29 Dec. 1945

Dear Lurton;

Forgive me for not writing sooner. But I have been in quite a spin trying to get squared around and in shape to go to work-and I mean go to work. Lurton, you are about to experience, come February or sooner, a flood of copy. You will have to hire squads of messengers just to get it around and an armored car just to pick up checks. . . .

Wednesday next will be delivered two Soundscriber recorders and one transcriber and a thousand records. I shall call hither and yon and get me a typist . . . These new Dictaphones are wonderful and even with the old ones I could roll out a volume. . . .

I wired you a couple weeks ago that I would take on the 49[1] book if you had an advance and a decent contract. Maybe you didn't receive the wire, for I haven't heard from you. Anyway, I will, for with my setup I can chew one off fast, the research data being plentiful in this locale and in my files. . . .

As you know, I roll enough copy in ordinary times so that sales operate as a sort of criticism service all its own. I know where I am going over well by sales. I very much need you for two vital purposes: to act as a bumper for rejects, to keep selling as only you can sell. This, I think, will answer its own question after we have been going for a while. . . .

The part of your opinion which I value highly is that steering ability into markets. You and I know that this business of openings for certain stories is overvalued. Competition, to really good yarns, is never very serious. No writer who is serious about it and who writes well has much competition. You can tell me, from what you are receiving from me, what markets I should try next, in what lengths. I like to write long stuff. Short stories pave the road to the poorhouse. Serials are covers. With my present setup I can roll the long stuff easily.

I am going, at first, into a small circle of writing. Novelettes thrust in succession into several fields just to orient myself. I used to be in DFW[2], BLACK MASK,[3] WESTERN STORY, air-war, adventure, sea, fantasy, etc., books. I may try again for those markets in rotation just to see where I come out best and get into swing. Then I want to go serial. Rog Terrill will buy. Jack Byrne, Jack Burr, John Campbell, etc., will buy if they get a special play on each story from you (for otherwise they will think I've turned my back on them, finding my stuff buried or unmentioned by phone). Then maybe we try some slick. Some serials. . . .

Now, one thing, a promise requested before I close. I always wrote straight at my editors, seldom missed, habituated them to a lot of fanfare and showmanship about stories. When you start to get volume from me, please promise me you'll phone the editor for whom the manuscript is intended and tell him you are sending it over, making him understand it's especially for him. Otherwise my old boys, who've stood by these many years, are going to wonder what they did to make me mad at them, for the relationship in almost every instance is quite personal and deep. Please?

Best regards,

Ron

1. 49: Reference to the upcoming 1949
   celebration of the California centennial.
2. DFW: Detective Fiction Weekly magazine.
3. Black Mask: a detective magazine.

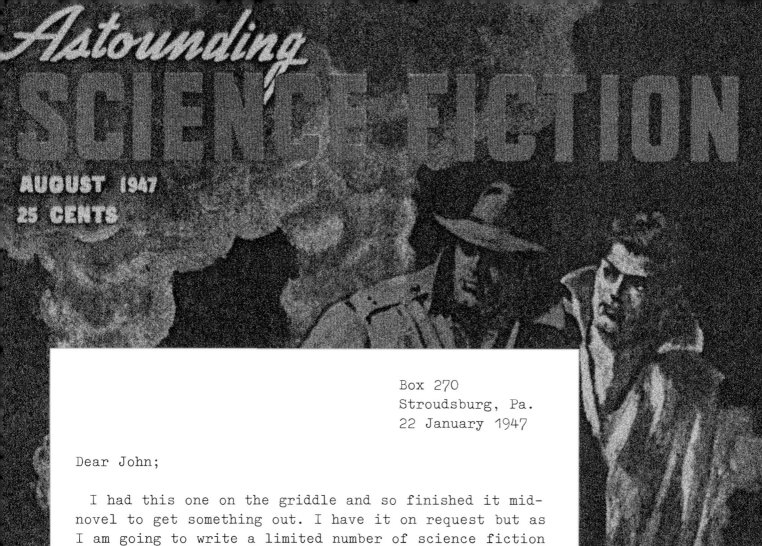

Astounding
SCIENCE FICTION
AUGUST 1947
25 CENTS

Box 270
Stroudsburg, Pa.
22 January 1947

Dear John;

I had this one on the griddle and so finished it mid-
novel to get something out. I have it on request but as
I am going to write a limited number of science fiction
stories this year, I see no reason to run a name which
in this field is essentially ASTOUNDING into competition
with you. The house requesting is a detective outlet for
me primarily and I would just as soon keep it so. I
get, by the way, good rates on why-do-they-have-to-do-
its which is a shocking commentary on the bloody,
vengeful mindedness of our citizens and precious public,
who ought to content themselves with good clean opera.
While I am writing otherwise, the house in question is
struggling to get me out the list of taboos I ordered
from them. By mid-February they will probably have
whipped me up some fine plots! Remember?

The novel is coming right along. The scientist will
save the world yet!

Cheers.

Ron

BY L. RON HUBBARD
THE END IS NOT YET

82

                                    Box 224
                                    Port Orchard, Wash.
                                    September 8, 1947

Dear Leo;

   Thank you for the check and the very pleasant letter. I have been
sitting here in the darnedest rainstorm I've seen since Alaska and this
was a beam of sunshine in an otherwise drab atmosphere. I am getting
terribly bored with this climate now that winter approaches and think I
had better load up my trailer and tow south. I have an aluminum job
which is tricked up as a writing office-nice mahogany desk, book cases,
patent chair, typewriter and Dictaphone stand-and it sure saves me a lot
of writing time. The rig has paid for itself a couple times, I think.
   The place I had down in Southern Calif. has been sold through my usual
lack of business acumen and I shall probably have a lot of trouble
buying another, for they say real estate there has just begun to boom.
But my aching bones are worth a lot to me, somehow, and so I shall have
to put up with being robbed, for the sake of sunlight.
   I'm doing a long novel in fits and starts for slick and have to have
it done by December because of tying it in with the California centennial
in '49. So I shall pause in the Mother Lode country a moment to check
some data and then go on south.
   Happen to notice you occasionally publish gold rush yarns in your
various westerns. Might unreel one from all this excess data. I am not
particularly happy about stacking up material and then not using it, but
I don't know that you would be interested.
   I note what you say about a 40,000-worder and as the length is an easy
one, we might see what can be done. I looked over some Startlings[1] I had
here and will check over the two you are sending.
   The story I have in mind is, so far, nameless, but it may please you.
   This letter has been slightly delayed due to my preoccupation in
starting on my trip.
   I am en route to California as I write. . . .
   A partial synopsis of BLACK TOWERS OF FEAR is enclosed. A fast report
on it will aid my work schedule.
   A possible writing schedule is also enclosed on which I would like your
comment. This may or may not make sense with your inventory or desires
but here it is. I like variety because it seems to keep me fresh in each
field. I can schedule this because, with returning health, I can
reestablish my wordage on its old basis.
   I would very much value your opinion on the synopsis and the schedule
and look forward to hearing from you.

                              My very best regards,

                              Ron

---

1. Startling: a science fiction magazine.

Box 297
No. Hollywood,
California
28 December 1947

John W. Campbell, Jr.
Street and Smith
122 E. 42nd St.
New York City 17, NY

Dear John;

On the second of November I sent an "Ole Doc" story to you and to date I have had no correspondence concerning it. I am writing to you because I am concerned for fear my mail to you is going astray somehow. If the story is under consideration it is perfectly all right of course. I am just anxious to know whether or not it ever got there.

Also, sometime in November (I don't have the exact date) I sent you a letter asking for a formal release of the copyrights Street and Smith holds on my stories so that I may get them printed in book form. I have had no answer to this either.

Since the prolonged silence on these two (well over a month on both of them) I am just a little bit suspicious that my mail to you has not been going through with the efficiency which our Post Office customarily gives to documents entrusted to its loving care. There is also the possibility that you do not have my address correctly.

If you just haven't gotten around to these things consider this letter just a hello. But, if there has been some slip up I would appreciate knowing about it[1].

My very, very best to you for the coming year, John.

Sincerely,

Ron

1. As LRH surmised, his third in the Ole Doc Methuselah series, "Her Majesty's Aberration," had been briefly misplaced in the mail. The work eventually appeared, however, in the March 1948 issue of *Astounding Science Fiction*.

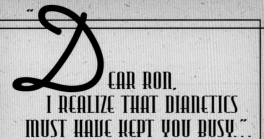

"DEAR RON, I REALIZE THAT DIANETICS MUST HAVE KEPT YOU BUSY..."

Beyond the spring of 1948, LRH correspondence with the publishing realm becomes virtually one-sided. That is, while the likes of a Sam Merwin, Jr. at *Standard Magazines* still regularly called for L. Ron Hubbard fiction, Ron's typical reply was but a cursory note attached to a submitted manuscript. The reason for such brevity is not hard to figure. Although he still managed to meet editorial demands, the sheer intensity of research towards the founding of Dianetics gave him little time for editorial discussion. Hence, Merwin's gentle nudge, "let's hear from you soon," while Martin Greenberg so rightly surmised, "I realize that Dianetics must have kept you busy . . ."

Lest one miss the larger point, however, LRH output from this period never actually flagged for a moment. As a matter of fact, a chronology of published works between that spring of 1948 and the autumn of 1950 reveals some forty novelettes and short stories. Moreover, those forty titles include such fully memorable tales as the deeply moving TO THE STARS—among the most widely reprinted short works of science fiction in the whole of the genre—and "Hoss Tamer," later inspiration for a teleplay of the same name and aired on NBC's *Tales of Wells Fargo*.

STANDARD MAGAZINES, Inc.
BETTER PUBLICATIONS, Inc.
10 EAST 40th, NEW YORK 16. NY
Leo Margulies, Editorial Director

June 18, 1948

Mr. L. Ron Hubbard
Box 297
North Hollywood,
California

Dear Ron:

How about some more stories from your gifted typewriter—either under the LaFayette byline?

We need material at almost any length up to 20,000 words, since again we have enlarged the Science Fiction magazines.

Let's hear from you soon.

Sincerely,

Sam Merwin, Jr.
Science Fiction Editor

TYPEWRITER
IN THE SKY

An Adventure in Time by
L. RON HUBBARD

GNOME PRESS
421 Claremont Parkway
New York 57, NY

August 15, 1950

My dear Ron:

   As you will note by the date on the check I have been holding it for some time. I
regret the delay but didn't know how to get in touch with you. Joe gave me your address
and I mislaid it till now. So here is the check for the story I used in my anthology.
   I have been waiting for a manuscript for "Typewriter in the Sky." I realize that
Dianetics must have kept you busy and no doubt still is. I have a lot of orders for
the book and it was originally scheduled for this past spring. I delayed the book and
it is scheduled for January publication and I need a manuscript....
   If you have the time I would like you to give me a call. I will be at this number
till next Monday any evening LUdlow 3-0965 or if you can give me a number where I can
call you I will do so....

                         Cordially,

                         Martin Greenberg

THE LETTERS TO ROBERT HEINLEIN

With L. Ron Hubbard's resumption of a literary life in 1980, came what critics would legitimately describe as a master's return in genuinely grand style. The statement cannot be overstressed, for nary an author in the whole of modern literature has managed a feat equivalent to a *Battlefield Earth* and a *Mission Earth*. After a three decade hiatus from the field came L. Ron Hubbard with the first works of science fiction to attract a truly mainstream readership in almost as many years—works with more than twelve million cumulative sales across a dozen languages, and of such continuing relevance the word *classic* is the only appropriate term. That longtime friend and fellow giant Robert Heinlein had stood so firmly by is also fully appropriate; for to name a work of similar stature one must return to his 1961 *Stranger in a Strange Land*.

L. Ron Hubbard   26 October 80

Dear Bob,

Congratulations on your new book, <u>The</u> <u>Number</u> <u>of</u> <u>the</u> <u>Beast</u> published by Fawcett Columbine. I read it with considerable pleasure. The old master has lost none of his touch. Indeed, he has added to it!

It do look like us old codgers sitting around the stove at the general store, still have more git up and go than them young fellers.

I have just finished a novel myself. It hasn't been shipped out yet but it's all done! I had a couple of months idle and so I rolled up my cuffs and wrote "Man: the Endangered Species."[1] That, at least, was the working title. It is 428,750 words long plus intro and is pure SF genre but in a modernized style and very fast-paced.

I said some nice things about you in the dedication and intro. I hope you do not mind and hope also that you can still blush! If such fills your modesty with horror, write back....

Anyway, it's a good thing for the field and fans we're still around. From other things on the stands, if 'tweren't for us, they wouldn't be readin' anything at all!

It is amusing that us, in our decrepit conditions, should still be outliving and out-producing the young fellers. Do you suppose it's the fallout? Or maybe the water? Or is it because we're just too cussed to move over and let somebody else on the bridge?

More power to you, dear Bob.

                                    Your friend,

                                    Ron

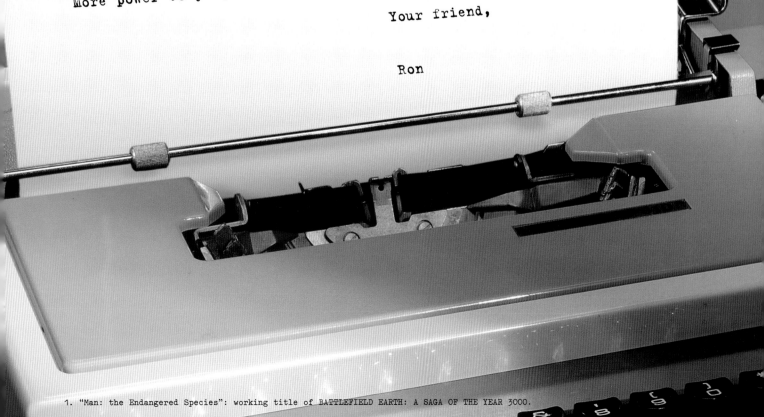

1. "Man: the Endangered Species": working title of BATTLEFIELD EARTH: A SAGA OF THE YEAR 3000.

15 December 1980

Dear Ron,

Thanks for the very nice note and for three (!) Xmas cards. I want to be on the lookout for your new SF novel. Will you please let me know the published title, date of publication, and publisher as soon as you know it yourself?

It has been a bit over forty years since you published FINAL BLACKOUT—but the warnings in it are more timely than ever.

I hope this finds you and yours well and happy and no longer hassled by the busies.

All the best!
Bob

Robert Heinlein

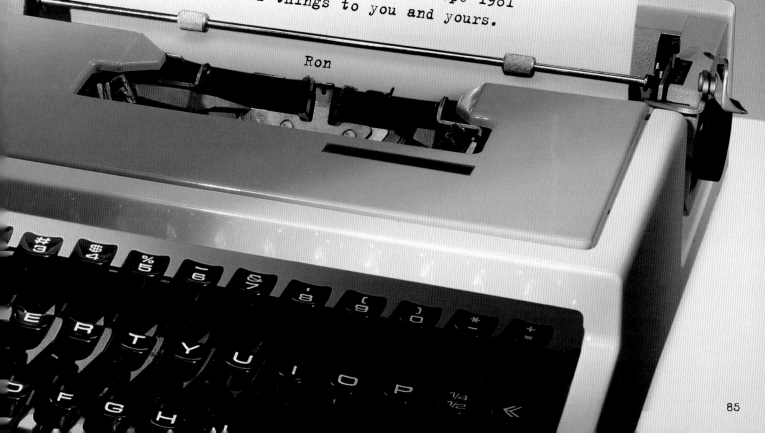

L. Ron Hubbard

24 December 1980

Dear Bob,

Very glad to hear from you. I hope you are getting yourself well "holiday'd" 'round about now. You surely will be informed of the published title and all the details, as soon as I have them. I'll send along a copy, too, as soon as I have one to send.

Yes, over forty years since FINAL BLACKOUT. Now they're accusing us old timers of being fortune-tellers of the future. I'm glad they've come to that, actually.

This year I celebrated 50 years at the old mill and so this is my commemoration piece to the occupation and my friends in it.

I hope you enjoy it and thanks for all your good wishes.

All the best to you too, Bob. I hope 1981 brings wonderful things to you and yours.

Ron

Epilogue

"In writing an adventure story a writer has to know
that he is adventuring for a lot of people who cannot.
The writer has to take them here and there about the globe
and show them excitement and love and realism."

— L.R.H.

Photograph by L. Ron Hubbard

"If you adventure
through life, you have
a good chance to be a
success on paper.
"Adventure doesn't
mean globetrotting,
exactly, and it doesn't
mean great deeds.
Adventuring is like art.
You have to live it
to make it real."

\- L. Ron Hubbard